CHRISTMAS RECIPES

The Best Christmas Holiday Cookbook

(Delicious Christmas & New Year Recipes, Complete Cookbook)

Patricia Everett

Published by Alex Howard

© Patricia Everett

All Rights Reserved

Christmas Recipes: The Best Christmas Holiday Cookbook (Delicious Christmas & New Year Recipes, Complete Cookbook)

ISBN 978-1-990169-49-6

All rights reserved. No part of this guide may be reproduced in any form without permission in writing from the publisher except in the case of brief quotations embodied in critical articles or reviews.

Legal & Disclaimer

The information contained in this book is not designed to replace or take the place of any form of medicine or professional medical advice. The information in this book has been provided for educational and entertainment purposes only.

The information contained in this book has been compiled from sources deemed reliable, and it is accurate to the best of the Author's knowledge; however, the Author cannot guarantee its accuracy and validity and cannot be held liable for any errors or omissions. Changes are periodically made to this book. You must consult your doctor or get professional medical advice before using any of the suggested remedies, techniques, or information in this book.

Table of contents

PART 1 INTRODUCTION 1

INTRODUCTION 2

Keto Brie Cranberry Festive Cups 3
Cheesy Bacon Zucchini Skins 6
Cheesy Cauliflower Breadsticks 8
PIZZA STUFFED MUSHROOMS 10
Cranberry and Cream Cheese Dip 12
Ranch Cauliflower Bites 14
Spinach Dip Stuffed Mushrooms 15
Blue Cheese Bacon Stuffed Peppers 17
Buffalo Chicken Meatballs 19
Low Carb Gluten Free Cranberry Bread 21
Bacon and Eggs Casserole 23
Blueberry Scones 25
Eggnog Scones 27
Gingerbread Fat Bombs Recipe 29
Ham & Cheese Omelet Roll 31
Low Carb Almond Flour Biscotti Paleo Sugarfree 33
Low Carb Santa Pancake 36
Christmas Breakfast Casserole 39
Peppermint Cream Frosted Ginger Cookies 41
Paleo Iced Gingerbread Cookies 44
Brandy Low Carb Pecan Pie 47
Ketogenic Trifle A Very Keto Christmas 49
Peanut Butter Chocolate French Silk Pie 51
Creme de Menthe Cream Puff Tree 54
Brussels Sprouts Gratin 57
Walnut Filled Pillows 59
Almond Joy Cookies Low Carb Sugar Free Thms 61
Baklava Cookies Low Carb Gluten Free 63
Easy Sugarfree Oatmeal Cookies Low Carb Glutenfree 65
Iced Lemon Cookies Low Carb Grain Sugar Free THM S 67

LOW CARB ALMOND FLOUR COOKIES RECIPE GLUTENFREE SHORTBREAD COOKIES 4 INGREDIENTS 69
SUGARFREE GINGERBREAD COOKIES LOW CARB PALEO 71
TAGALONG PEANUT BUTTER COOKIE BARS 73
CRANBERRY GINGER BUTTER COOKIES LOW CARB AND GLUTEN FREE 75
3-INGREDIENT CHOCOLATE MOUSSE LOW CARB 77
CHOCOLATE CHAMPAGNE CUPCAKES WITH RASPBERRY ICING 79
CHOCOLATE FUDGE KETO COOKIES 81
KENTUCKY BUTTER CAKE 83
KETO CHOCOLATE SALAMI 85
LAVA CAKE FOR 1 LOW CARB 87
LOW CARB CHRISTMAS PUDDING 89
MAPLE MACADAMIA NUT COOKIES 91
SOUR CREAM CAKE 93
CREAM CHEESE COOKIES GLUTEN FREE 96
GLUTEN FREE THUMBPRINT COOKIES WITH JAM 98
GRAINFREE SPICE COOKIES AUTOIMMUNE PALEO VEGAN 100
NO BAKE COCONUT COOKIES COCONUT DELIGHTS SUGAR DAIRY EGG AND GRAIN FREE ... 102
PUMPKIN SNICKER DOODLES GLUTEN DAIRY SUGAR FREE W VEGAN GRAIN FREE OPTIONS . 104
SNICKERDOODLE COOKIE DOUGH BITES PALEO GRAIN FREE EGG FREE LOW CARB 107
BAKLAVA TARTLETS 109
SEAFOOD GUMBO 111
NEW ORLEANS STYLE SPICY SHRIMP 113
HAM PINEAPPLE KABOBS 115
GINGERBREAD SPICE COFFEE RECIPE 117
LOW CARB CHOCOLATE PEPPERMINT COCKTAIL 119
LOW CARB SANTA COCKTAIL 121

PART 2 123

CHRISTMAS BISCUITS 124
MAGICAL SUGAR COOKIES 126
MOCHA MEN AND STAR COOKIES 128
SOFT CHOCOLATE CHIP COOKIES 130
CHOCOLATE PEPPERMINT PINWHEEL COOKIES 132
THE MOST WONDERFUL GINGERBREAD COOKIES 134
CHEWY CHOCOLATE CHIP OATMEAL COOKIES 137

Uncle Bill's Whipped Shortbread Cookies	139
Pecan Puffs	141
Christmas Chocolate Cherry Cookies	143
White Chocolate Chip Cranberry Oatmeal Cookies	145
Peanut Butter Blossoms	147
Penguin Cookies	149
Caramel Macchiato Cookies	151
Chocolate Crinkle Peppermint Blossom	153
Triple Chocolate Peppermint Cookies	155
Christmas Sugar Cookie Recipe	156
Peppermint Twist Macarons	157
Turtle Snickerdoodles	160
Black-And-White Cookies	162
Anise-Almond Sprinkle Cookies	164
Gingerbread Cookies	165
Cherry Snowball Cookies	166
Norwegian Wafer Cookies	167
Meringue Cookies	168
Chocolate Almond Crisps	169
Italian Christmas Cookies	170
The Bestest Butter Cookies	171
Christmas Mint Cookies	172
Raspberry Swirl Cookies	173
Elaine's Holiday Cut Out Sugar Cookies	174
Peppermint Christmas Cookies	175
Christmas Gingerbread Cookies	176
Cake Mix Christmas Cookies	178
Jam-Filled Christmas Cookies	179
Melomakarona (A Greek Christmas Cookie)	180
Christmas Gingerbread Cookies	182
Swedish Christmas Cookies	183
Gluten-Free Chocolate Chip Cookies	184
Gluten Free Dutch Sugar Cookies	185
Flourless Chocolate Snowball Cookies	187
Oatmeal Lace Cookies	188
Chocolate Almond Crisps	189

Gingerbread Cookies (Gluten Free) 190

Part 1

Introduction

The holidays are here! Unlike Thanksgiving, you get much more flexibility in terms of dinner. Tired of turkey? We are too, that's why we're exploring our options this year! Check out our top contenders for this year's feast. We gathered the greatest holiday recipes from around the blogosphere that we think would go great on our table (and in our bellies).

With keto-friendly, whole-food based recipes that you will use year after year to impress your guests, and stay keto throughout the holiday season. Featuring a variety of over 100 low-carb appetizers, starter, side dish, entree, dessert, and condiment recipes, each dish will bring your holiday meals to life, whether you're hosting a group with food allergies, your keto friends, or non-ketoers.

Keto Brie Cranberry Festive Cups

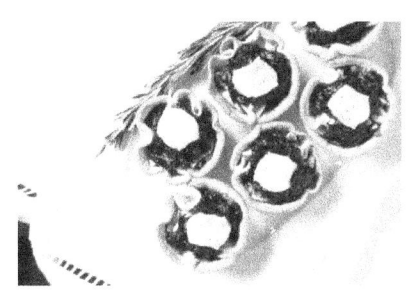

"These keto brie cranberry cups make for one killer holiday entree. Think oozing brie, topped with our deliciously sweet and tangy cranberry relish, crunchy pecans, and aromatic rosemary. All wrapped up in one killer (and easy peasy!) dough."

Serving: 6 cups | Ready in: 15 m

Ingredients:

- 96 g almond flour
- 24 g coconut flour
- 2 teaspoons xanthan gum
- 1 teaspoon baking powder
- 1/8-1/4 teaspoon kosher salt (depending on whether sweet or savory)
- 2 teaspoons apple cider vinegar
- 1 egg (lightly beaten)
- 3 teaspoons water
- 1 5-inch wheel brie cheese (diced)
- 40 g roughly chopped pecans
- 1 tablespoon very finely minced rosemary
- 100 g keto cranberry relish (or cranberry sauce of choice)

- **arugula**
- extra virgin olive oil (to taste)
- balsamic vinegar (to taste)

Direction:

1. Add almond flour, coconut flour, xanthan gum, baking powder and salt to food processor. Pulse until thoroughly combined.

2. Pour in apple cider vinegar with the food processor running. Once it has distributed evenly, pour in the egg. Followed by the water. Stop the food processor once the dough forms into a ball. The dough will be sticky to touch.

3. Wrap dough in cling film and knead it through the plastic for a minute or two. Think of it a bit like a stress ball. Allow dough to rest for 10 minutes (and up to two days in the fridge).

4. Break the dough into eight 1" balls (26g a piece). Roll out between two sheets of parchment or waxed paper with a rolling pin or using a tortilla press. If fuzzy about presentation, trim edges. The dough recipe (inevitably) makes a bit extra, so we suggest turning it into crackers.

5. Preheat oven to 350°F/180°C.

6. Fit pastry rounds onto a muffin tray. Fill with brie, pecans, rosemary, cranberry relish, and brie again. Finish off with freshly ground black pepper to taste.

7. Bake for 10-16 minutes (depending on thickness), until pastry is golden and cheese is fully melted. Keep an eye on them, as coconut flour has the tendency to suddenly brown very quickly! Serve right away.

8. These guys are best served warm and straight from the oven, but they also do re-warm quite well.

9. Note that you can assemble the cups a day before, wrap the muffin tray with cling film, and bake straight from the fridge as needed.

Nutrition Information:
- Calories: 89 kcal
- Total Fat: 6 g
- Saturated Fat: 1 g
- Cholesterol: 20 mg
- Sodium: 51 mg
- Total Carbohydrate: 4 g
- Protein: 3 g
- Fiber: 2 g

Cheesy Bacon Zucchini Skins

"Cheesy Bacon Zucchini Skins loaded with Monterey Jack cheese, bacon, green onion, and dipped in sour cream - these are the low carb version of potato skins you've been looking for!"

Serving: 12 zucchini skins | Ready in: 20 m

Ingredients:
- 6 slices bacon
- 3 medium zucchini
- 1 cup Monterey Jack cheese (shredded)
- 3 green onions (sliced)
- 1 cup sour cream

Direction:
1. Chop bacon and saute in a frying pan over medium heat until crispy, drain on paper towels.
2. Slice zucchini in half length-wise. Cut in half and cut off the ends, creating 4 skins from each zucchini, 12 skins total.
3. Using a large spoon, firmly scoop out the white part of the zucchini leaving about 1/4" inside the skins. Discard zucchini insides and place skins cut side up on a large cookie sheet.

4. Sprinkle evenly with cheese and crumbled bacon. Bake at 400 degrees for 5 - 10 minutes or until cheese is done and zucchini is just slightly soft (they should still have a slight raw crunch to them).
5. Allow to cool 5 minutes before topping with green onion and serving with sour cream or ranch dressing to dip.

Nutrition Information:
- Calories: 127 kcal
- Total Fat: 11 g
- Saturated Fat: 5 g
- Cholesterol: 25 mg
- Sodium: 143 mg
- Total Carbohydrate: 2 g
- Protein: 4 g
- Sugar: 1 g

Cheesy Cauliflower Breadsticks

"These Cheesy Cauliflower Breadsticks are gluten free, low carb and so delicious! Use this crust for breadsticks or for pizza. This recipe is a winner and a keeper!"

Serving: 8 | Ready in: 50 m

Ingredients:

- 4 cups cauliflower (riced, about 1 large head of cauliflower)
- 4 eggs
- 2 cups mozzarella cheese
- 3 tsp oregano
- 4 cloves garlic (minced)
- salt and pepper to taste
- 1 cup mozzarella cheese (or more, for topping)

Direction:

1. Preheat oven to 425 F degrees. Prepare 2 pizza dishes or a large baking sheet with parchment paper.
2. Make sure your cauliflower is roughly chopped in florets. Add the florets to your food processor and pulse until cauliflower resembles rice.
3. Place the cauliflower in a microwavable container and cover with lid. Microwave for 10 minutes. Let the cauliflower cool

just until there's no more steam coming from it. Place the microwaved cauliflower in a large
bowl and add the eggs, 2 cups of mozzarella, oregano, garlic, salt and pepper. Mix everything together.
4. Separate the mixture in two and place each half onto the prepared baking sheets and shape into either a pizza crust, or a rectangular shape for the breadsticks.
5. Bake the crust (no topping yet) for about 25 minutes or until nice and golden. Don't be afraid the crust is not soggy at all. Once golden, sprinkle with remaining mozzarella cheese and put back in the oven for another 5 minutes or until cheese has melted.
6. Slice and serve.

Nutrition Information:
- Calories: 174 kcal
- Total Fat: 11 g
- Saturated Fat: 6 g
- Cholesterol: 115 mg
- Sodium: 310 mg
- Total Carbohydrate: 4 g
- Protein: 13 g
- Fiber: 1 g
- Sugar: 1 g

PIZZA STUFFED MUSHROOMS

"I love stuffed mushrooms... any kind. Cream cheese, cheese & bacon, crab, cheeseburger stuffed or even a simple salsa... it doesn't matter what you put in them, it's always the appetizer I go for first!"

Ready in: 25 m

Ingredients:
- 24 mushrooms
- 1 clove garlic
- 2 teaspoons olive oil
- 1 can pizza sauce
- mozzarella cheese
- mini pepperoni (or your favorite toppings)
- basil for serving

Direction:
1. Preheat oven to 375 degrees.
2. Clean mushrooms and remove stems. Using a small spoon, scoop out insides of mushrooms to allow enough room for filling.

3. Finely chop mushroom stems. Add olive oil, garlic and chopped mushroom stem to a pan over medium heat. Cook 5 minutes cool slightly.
4. Stuff mushroom stems in mushroom caps. Top each with 1 tablespoon pizza sauce, 1 tablespoon cheese and 3 mini pepperonis.
5. Bake 18-20 minutes or until mushrooms are cooked and cheese is browned and bubbly.
6. Cool slightly before serving.

Nutrition Information:
- Calories: 181 kcal
- Total Fat: 9 g
- Saturated Fat: 1 g
- Sodium: 29 mg
- Total Carbohydrate: 16 g
- Protein: 15 g
- Fiber: 4 g
- Sugar: 9 g

Cranberry and Cream Cheese Dip

Serving: 8 | Ready in: 10 m

Ingredients:
- 12 oz fresh cranberries
- 2 jalapeños (deseeded)
- ¼ cup fresh cilantro
- ¼ cup low carb sweetener (eg xylitol or Swerve)
- 1 tsp lemon juice
- 16 oz cream cheese (room temperature)

Direction:
1. Add the cranberries, jalapeños and cilantro to a food processor and pulse a few times.
2. Add the lemon juice and sweetener, then pulse again until everything is finely chopped. Transfer to a bowl and keep in the fridge until required.
3. To serve, spread the cream cheese onto a plate, then spoon the cranberry mixture on top.
4. Garnish with fresh cilantro.

Nutrition Information:

- Calories: 215 kcal
- Total Fat: 19 g
- Saturated Fat: 10 g
- Cholesterol: 62 mg
- Sodium: 183 mg
- Total Carbohydrate: 8 g
- Protein: 3 g
- Fiber: 2 g
- Sugar: 3 g

Ranch Cauliflower Bites

"Check out this recipe for extremely addictive bacon ranch cauliflower bites from Delish.com."

Serving: 18 | Ready in: 30 m

Ingredients:
- 1 head of cauliflower
- 2 large eggs
- 1 packet ranch seasoning mix
- 1 1/4 shredded sharp cheddar cheese, divided into 1 c and 1/4 c
- 6 strips bacon, cooked and crumbled
- 1 tsp. chives, plus more for topping

Direction:
1. Preheat oven to 375 degrees F. Pulse cauliflower in a food processor until it forms large crumbs. Place cauliflower in paper towels or cheesecloth and wring out any excess water. Pour cauliflower crumbles into a large bowl. Add eggs, 1 c cheese, ranch seasoning, about 3/4s of the bacon, and chives. Spritz a muffin tin with cooking spray, then fill each one about 2/3s full. Top with a sprinkle of cheese and crumbled bacon. Bake for about 20-22 minutes, or until lightly golden. Garnish with additional chives before serving.

Spinach DipStuffed Mushrooms

"I use a melon baller to hollow out the mushroom caps to make them easier to stuff. They also fit neatly into muffin tins or a deviled egg tray for traveling. Ashley Pierce, Brantford, Ontario"

Serving: 16 appetizers. | Ready in: 40 m

Ingredients:
- 16 large fresh mushrooms (about 1-1/2 pounds)
- 1 tablespoon olive oil
- 2 cups fresh baby spinach, coarsely chopped
- 2 garlic cloves, minced
- 1/2 cup reduced-fat sour cream
- 3 ounces reduced-fat cream cheese
- 1/3 cup shredded part-skim mozzarella cheese
- 3 tablespoons grated Parmesan cheese
- 1/4 teaspoon salt
- 1/4 teaspoon cayenne pepper
- 1/4 teaspoon pepper

Direction:

1. Preheat oven to 400degrees. Remove stems from mushrooms and set caps aside; discard stems or save for another use. In a small skillet, heat olive oil over medium heat. Add spinach; saute until wilted. Add garlic;
cook 1 minute longer., Combine spinach mixture with remaining ingredients. Stuff into mushroom caps. Place in a 15x10-in. baking pan coated with cooking spray. Bake, uncovered, until mushrooms are tender, 12-15 minutes. Serve warm.

Nutrition Information:
- Calories: 44 calories
- Total Fat: 3g fat (2g saturated fat)
- Cholesterol: 9mg cholesterol
- Sodium: 100mg sodium
- Total Carbohydrate: 1g carbohydrate (1g sugars
- Protein: 2g protein.
- Fiber: 0 fiber) g

Blue Cheese Bacon Stuffed Peppers

"Whenever I put out a plate of these cute little appetizers, people come flocking. Good thing there are lots of peppers in each bag. Tara Cruz, Kersey, Colorado"

Serving: 1 dozen. | Ready in: 20 m

Ingredients:
- 3 medium sweet yellow, orange or red peppers
- 4 ounces cream cheese, softened
- 1/2 cup crumbled blue cheese
- 3 bacon strips, cooked and crumbled
- 1 green onion, thinly sliced

Direction:
1. Cut peppers into quarters. Remove and discard stems and seeds. In a small bowl, mix cream cheese, blue cheese, bacon and green onion until blended., Grill peppers, covered, over medium-high heat or broil 4 in. from heat 2-3 minutes on each side or until slightly charred.

2. Remove peppers from grill; fill each with about 1 tablespoon cheese mixture. Grill 2-3 minutes longer or until cheese is melted.

Nutrition Information:
- Calories: 73 calories
- Total Fat: 6g fat (3g saturated fat)
- Cholesterol: 17mg cholesterol
- Sodium: 136mg sodium
- Total Carbohydrate: 3g carbohydrate (0 sugars)
- Protein: 3g protein.
- Fiber: 0 fiber g

Buffalo Chicken Meatballs

"I like to dunk these appetizer meatballs in blue cheese or ranch salad dressing. If I make them for a meal, I often skip the dressing and serve with blue cheese polenta on the side. Amber Massey, Argyle, Texas"

Serving: 2 dozen. | Ready in: 35 m

Ingredients:
- 3/4 cup panko (Japanese) bread crumbs
- 1/3 cup plus 1/2 cup Louisiana-style hot sauce, divided
- 1/4 cup chopped celery
- 1 large egg white
- 1 pound lean ground chicken
- Reduced-fat blue cheese or ranch salad dressing, optional

Direction:
1. Preheat oven to 400 deg;. In a large bowl, combine bread crumbs, 1/3 cup hot sauce, celery and egg white.
2. Add chicken; mix lightly but thoroughly., Shape into twenty-four 1-in. balls. Place on a greased rack in a shallow baking pan.

3. Bake 20-25 minutes or until cooked through., Toss meatballs with remaining hot sauce. If desired, drizzle with salad dressing just before serving.

Nutrition Information:
- Calories: 35 calories
- Total Fat: 1g fat (0 saturated fat)
- Cholesterol: 14mg cholesterol
- Sodium: 24mg sodium
- Total Carbohydrate: 2g carbohydrate (0 sugars
- Protein: 4g protein.
- Fiber: 0 fiber g

Low Carb Gluten Free Cranberry Bread

"A delicious gluten free low carb cranberry bread with fresh cranberries. This sugar-free bread uses a combination of stevia and erythritol sweeteners."

Serving: 12 people | Ready in: 85 m

Ingredients:

- 2 cups almond flour
- 1/2 cup powdered erythritol (or Swerve)
- 1/2 teaspoon Steviva stevia powder
- 1 1/2 teaspoons baking powder
- 1/2 teaspoon baking soda
- 1 teaspoon salt
- 4 tablespoons unsalted butter (melted (or coconut oil)
- 1 teaspoon blackstrap molasses (optional (for brown sugar flavor))
- 4 large eggs (at room temperature)
- 1/2 cup coconut milk
- 1 bag cranberries (12 ounces)

Direction:

1. Preheat oven to 350 degrees; grease a 9-by-5 inch loaf pan and set aside.

2. In a large bowl, whisk together flour, erythritol, stevia, baking powder, baking soda, and salt; set aside.
3. In a medium bowl, combine butter, molasses, eggs, and coconut milk.
4. Mix dry mixture into wet mixture to dry mixture until well combined.
5. Fold in cranberries. Pour batter into prepared pan.
6. Bake until a toothpick inserted in the center of the loaf comes clean, about 1 hour and 15 minutes.
7. Transfer pan to a wire rack; let bread cool 15 minutes before removing from pan.

Nutrition Information:
- Calories: 179 kcal
- Total Fat: 15 g
- Saturated Fat: 4 g
- Cholesterol: 72 mg
- Sodium: 276 mg
- Total Carbohydrate: 7 g
- Protein: 6.4 g
- Fiber: 2 g
- Sugar: 1 g

Bacon and Eggs Casserole

"Because it's fast to fix and such a great hit with family and friends, this bacon and eggs dish is a favorite of mine to make for brunches. Served with a fruit salad, hot muffins and croissants, this bacon and eggs casserole is excellent for an after-church brunch. Deanna Durward-Orr, Windsor, Ontario"

Serving: 10 servings. | Ready in: 60 m

Ingredients:
- 4 bacon strips
- 18 large Nellie's Free Range Eggs
- 1 cup whole milk
- 1 cup shredded cheddar cheese
- 1 cup sour cream
- 1/4 cup sliced green onions
- 1 to 1-1/2 teaspoons salt
- 1/2 teaspoon pepper

Direction:
1. In a large skillet, cook bacon over medium heat until crisp. Remove to paper towel to drain., In a large bowl, beat eggs. Add milk, cheese, sour cream, onions, salt and pepper., Pour into a greased 13x9-in. baking dish.

2. Crumble bacon and sprinkle on top. Bake, uncovered, at 325 for 40-45 minutes or until knife inserted in center comes out clean. Let stand for 5 minutes.

Nutrition Information:
- Calories: 289 calories
- Total Fat: 22g fat (10g saturated fat)
- Cholesterol: 420mg cholesterol
- Sodium: 508mg sodium
- Total Carbohydrate: 4g carbohydrate (3g sugars)
- Protein: 16g protein.
- Fiber: 0 fiber g

Blueberry Scones

"Low carb blueberry scones are a great low carb breakfast recipe to enjoy with a cup of tea!"

Serving: 8 | Ready in: 20 m

Ingredients:

- 1 c Blueberries (fresh)
- 1/2 c Coconut flour
- 1/2 c Almond flour
- 1/2 c Butter (unsalted, softened)
- 1/2 c Heavy cream
- 2 Eggs
- 5 Tbsp. Truvia
- 2 tsp Baking powder
- 2 tsp Vanilla extract
- 1/4 tsp Salt

Direction:

1. Preheat oven to 350°F
2. In a large bowl combine, all dry ingredients.
3. Stir in blueberries.

4. Add butter, heavy cream, eggs and vanilla extract and mix until well combined.

5. Using your hand, shape about 2 tablespoons of dough into a triangular shape. Place on cookie sheet and bake for 12-18 minutes or until outer edges are golden.
6. Let cool.
7. Store in an airtight container.
8. Makes about 8-10 scones.

Nutrition Information:
- Calories: 223 kcal
- Total Fat: 20g
- Saturated Fat: 5g
- Cholesterol: 67mg
- Sodium: 126mg
- Total Carbohydrate: 8g
- Protein: 3g
- Fiber: 3g
- Sugar: 3g

Eggnog Scones

"Get into the holiday spirit with these low carb eggnog scones. Such a festive keto breakfast treat!"

Serving: 8 scones | Ready in: 45 m

Ingredients:
- 2 cups almond flour
- 1/4 cup Swerve Sweetener
- 2 tsp baking powder
- 1/2 tsp ground nutmeg
- 1/2 tsp salt
- 1/2 cup sugar-free eggnog
- 1 large egg
- 1/2 tsp vanilla or rum extract
- 1/4 cup powdered Swerve Sweetener
- 2 tbsp sugar-free eggnog

Direction:
1. For the scones, combine flour, sugar, salt, and baking powder in a large mixing bowl. Add in butter (I used the

beater blade of my electric mixer, but you can use a pastry cutter).
2. Mix until it resembles coarse crumbs.
3. Add in egg, greek yogurt, eggnog, rum extract and nutmeg. Combine completely.
4. On a large baking sheet with parchment paper (or silpat), shape dough into a large rectangle using your hands. I dusted my hands and the dough with flour to keep it from sticking.
5. Press your rectangle to 8 1/2 inch x 6 1/2 inch- 1/2inch thick. Using a pizza cutter, slice in half horizontally. Then cut it into thirds vertically (you will have 6 rectangles). Cut each rectangle in half to make 2 triangles. You will be left with a total of 12 triangles. Don't separate them on the baking sheet yet.
6. Bake in a 350 degree oven for 25 minutes. Remove from oven and re-cut your triangles.
7. Separate carefully and return to oven for an additional 10 minutes. Remove and cool completely before applying glaze.
8. For the glaze, whisk together the sugar, eggnog and nutmeg. Add more/less eggnog for desired consistency. Spoon glaze over each scone and allow to set, about 20 minutes.
9. Store in an airtight container for up to 5 days. ENJOY.

Nutrition Information:
- Calories: 182 kcal
- Total Fat: 15.29 g
- Total Carbohydrate: 6.1 g
- Protein: 6.46 g
- Fiber: 3.03 g

Gingerbread Fat Bombs Recipe

"These fat bomb recipes have all of the flavors of a gingerbread cookie with none of the carbs. The best part is they are low carb and ready in 10 minutes!"

Serving: 16 | Ready in: 10 m

Ingredients:

- 2 cups Finely ground almond flour
- 2/3 cup Swerve sweetener
- 1 teaspoon Ground ginger
- 1/2 teaspoon Ground cinnamon
- 1/2 teaspoon Ground nutmeg
- 1/4 teaspoon Kosher salt
- 6 Tablespoons Melted butter
- 1 teaspoon Molasses (optional)

Direction:

1. Add all of the dry ingredients to a medium sized bowl and mix to combine. Stir in the melted butter and molasses to form a thick dough.

2. Using a small cookie scoop, scoop out a portion of dough and roll it into a ball. Place the balls in an air tight container and refrigerate for 1 hour.
3. Keep in the refrigerator for snacking! Makes 16 balls.

Nutrition Information:
- Calories: 120 kcal

Ham & Cheese Omelet Roll

"This brunch dish has easy ingredients and an impressive look all rolled into one! I love hosting brunch, and this special omelet roll is one of my very favorite items to prepare and share. A platter of these pretty swirled slices disappears fast. Nancy Daugherty, Portland, Ohio"

Serving: 12 servings. | Ready in: 50 m

Ingredients:
- 4 ounces cream cheese, softened
- 3/4 cup 2% milk
- 2 tablespoons all-purpose flour
- 1/4 teaspoon salt
- 12 large Nellie's Free Range Eggs
- 2 tablespoons Dijon mustard
- 2-1/4 cups shredded cheddar cheese, divided
- 2 cups finely chopped fully cooked ham
- 1/2 cup thinly sliced green onions

Direction:
1. Line the bottom and sides of a greased 15x10x1-in. baking pan with parchment paper; grease the paper and set aside.,

In a small bowl, beat cream cheese and milk until smooth. Add flour and salt; mix until combined. In a large bowl, whisk eggs until blended.
2. Add cream cheese mixture; mix well. Pour into prepared pan., Bake at 375deg; for 30-35 minutes or until eggs are puffed and set. Remove from the oven. Immediately spread with mustard and sprinkle with 1 cup cheese.
3. Sprinkle with ham, onions and 1 cup cheese., Roll up from a short side, peeling parchment paper away while rolling.
4. Sprinkle top of roll with the remaining cheese; bake 3-4 minutes longer or until cheese is melted.

Nutrition Information:
- Calories: 239 calories
- Total Fat: 17g fat (9g saturated fat)
- Cholesterol: 260mg cholesterol
- Sodium: 637mg sodium
- Total Carbohydrate: 4g carbohydrate (2g sugars)
- Protein: 17g protein.
- Fiber: 0 fiber g

Low Carb Almond Flour Biscotti Paleo Sugarfree

"This paleo, low carb biscotti recipe is prepared with almond flour. Now sugar-free, gluten-free biscotti can be made easy with only 6 ingredients!"

Serving: 16 biscotti | Ready in: 55 m

Ingredients:
- 2 cups Blanched almond flour
- 1/4 cup Erythritol (or any granular sweetener)
- 1 tsp Gluten-free baking powder
- 2 large Egg (beaten)
- 2 tbsp Coconut oil (measured solid, then melted; can also use butter instead)
- 1 tsp Almond extract

Direction:
1. Preheat the oven to 350 degrees F (177 degrees C). Line a baking sheet with parchment paper.
2. In a large bowl, combine the almond flour, erythritol, and baking powder. Stir in eggs to form a dough.

3. In a small bowl, combine the melted coconut oil and almond extract. Stir the mixture into the dough.
4. Form a wide, flattened log (like a flattened loaf shape) out of the dough on the lined baking sheet. It should be about 3/4 in tall, 4 in wide, and 7.5 in long (2 cm tall, 10 cm wide, 19 cm long) .
5. Bake for 20-30 minutes, until golden brown. The top should be firm but the inside is still a little soft at this point.
6. Allow the loaf to cool to room temperature, about 30-60 minutes, to allow it to firm up more. Toward the end, preheat the oven again, this time to 300 degrees F.
7. Use a sharp knife to carefully slice the loaf into individual biscotti (about 1/2" thick). A straight down movement works better than a see-saw motion, to avoid crumbling. Arrange in a single layer on the baking sheet (you may need two baking sheets for this). Handle the slices with care - they are fragile for now.
8. Bake on the second-from-the-top rack for 10-15 minutes, until bottom side is golden. Carefully flip the biscotti over (they'll still be soft and fragile). Bake for 8-12 more minutes, until other side is golden.
9. Leave the pan(s) in the oven. Turn off the heat and prop the door open with a wooden spoon. Allow to gradually cool completely in the oven, until crispy.

Nutrition Information:
- Calories: 106 kcal
- Total Fat: 9 g
- Saturated Fat: 2 g
- Cholesterol: 27 mg
- Sodium: 14 mg
- Total Carbohydrate: 3 g
- Protein: 4 g
- Fiber: 2 g

- Sugar: 1 g

Low Carb Santa Pancake

Serving: 2 | Ready in: 15 m

Ingredients:
- ½ cup low carb baking mix
- 1 tbs vegetable oil
- 1 egg (beaten)
- ⅓ cup unsweetened almond milk
- 1 tsp low carb sweetener (granular Swerve or similar)
- ¼ tsp baking powder
- ¼ tsp vanilla extract
- 10 strawberries (hulled and halved)
- 4 tbs dairy whipped cream
- 2 tbs low carb mini chocolate chips (eg Lily's or similar)

Direction:
1. Make the pancake batter by combining low carb baking mix, vegetable oil, a beaten egg, unsweetened almond milk, baking powder, sweetener and vanilla extract in a large bowl.
2. Heat a non-stick skillet and pour half the batter in. Let the base cook then flip it over.

3. When it is fully cooked, transfer it to a plate and add strawberries for a hat, whipped cream for the hat trim and beard, and chocolate chips for eyes and mouth. Keep it warm while you make the other pancake.

Nutrition Information:

- Calories: 275 kcal
- Total Fat: 14 g
- Saturated Fat: 8 g
- Cholesterol: 86 mg
- Sodium: 163 mg
- Total Carbohydrate: 20 g
- Protein: 15 g
- Fiber: 8 g
- Sugar: 2 g

Christmas Breakfast Casserole

"Spicy sausage, herbs and vegetables fill this casserole with hearty flavor. I like to make it for my family's Christmas breakfast, but it's delicious any time of day! Debbie Carter, O'Fallon, Illinois"

Serving: 12 servings. | Ready in: 45 m

Ingredients:
- 1 pound Johnsonville® Ground Mild Italian sausage
- 1 cup chopped onion
- 1 jar (7 ounces) roasted red peppers, drained and chopped, divided
- 1 package (10 ounces) frozen chopped spinach, thawed and well drained
- 1 cup all-purpose flour
- 1/4 cup grated Parmesan cheese
- 1 teaspoon dried basil
- 1/2 teaspoon salt
- 8 large eggs
- 2 cups whole milk
- 1 cup shredded provolone cheese

- Fresh rosemary sprigs, optional

    Direction:
1. Preheat oven to 425degrees. In a skillet, cook sausage and onion over medium heat until sausage is no longer pink; drain. Transfer to a greased 3-qt. baking dish.
2. Sprinkle with half of the red peppers and all the spinach., In a bowl, combine flour, Parmesan cheese, basil and salt. Combine eggs and milk; add to dry ingredients and mix well. Pour over spinach., Bake 20-25 minutes or until a knife inserted in the center comes out clean.
3. Sprinkle with provolone cheese and remaining red peppers. Bake 2 minutes longer or until cheese is melted. Let stand 5 minutes before cutting. Garnish with rosemary if desired.

Nutrition Information:
- Calories: 232 calories
- Total Fat: 13g fat (6g saturated fat)
- Cholesterol: 170mg cholesterol
- Sodium: 531mg sodium
- Total Carbohydrate: 13g carbohydrate (4g sugars)
- Protein: 14g protein.
- Fiber: 1g fiber

Peppermint Cream Frosted Ginger Cookies

"Peppermint Cream Ginger Cookies are low carb, paleo, and gluten free with a dairy free option. Soft spiced ginger cookie with a mint cream frosting."

Serving: 20 | Ready in: 21 m

Ingredients:
- 2 cups blanched almond flour
- ⅔ cup sweetener of choice: Swerve for low carb or coconut sugar for paleo
- 2 tsp ground ginger
- ½ tsp ground cinnamon
- ½ tsp nutmeg
- ⅛ tsp sea salt
- ½ tsp baking soda
- 6 tbsp butter (melted or 6 tbsp organic vegetable shortening (for dairy free))
- ½ tsp molasses or sugar free maple syrup
- 1 lg egg
- 2 tbsp water

- 4 ounces cream cheese (or ½ cup organic vegetable shortening (for dairy free or paleo))
- ¼ cup powdered sweetener of choice: Swerve confectioners for low carb (or coconut sugar (finely ground in magic bullet type blender) for paleo.)
- 2 tbsp heavy cream or coconut milk
- ⅛ tsp vanilla extract
- ½ tsp peppermint extract
- Optional Garnish: ¼ tsp allspice (nutmeg or ½ tbsp crushed sugar free peppermints)

Direction:

1. Preheat oven to 350 F (177 C), and line 2 baking sheets or one xl baking sheet with parchment paper.
2. In a large mixing bowl combine: almond flour, sweetener of choice, ground ginger, cinnamon, nutmeg, sea salt, and baking soda. Stir until combined. Set aside.
3. In a medium size mixing bowl combine: melted butter or shortening, molasses, and egg. Mix until combined.
4. Add the wet mixture to the dry mixture. Stir until combined.
5. Add water to the mixture and stir again until dough forms. Use a cookie scoop to tablespoon size scoops onto a baking sheet.
6. Using the back of a spoon or the palm of your hand, press cookies gently to flatten a little.
7. Bake at 350 F (177 C) for 11 to 15 minutes, or until outer edges under cookies are just browning. Remove from oven and cool before transferring to a wire rack or plate.
8. a stand mixer or hand mixer with bowl, combine all the frosting ingredients and mix until creamy.
9. Frost cookies and sprinkle with optional nutmeg or allspice.

Nutrition Information:
- Calories: 126 kcal

- Total Fat: 12 g
- Saturated Fat: 5 g
- Total Carbohydrate: 3 g
- Protein: 3 g
- Fiber: 1 g
- Sugar: 1 g

Paleo Iced Gingerbread Cookies

"A grain free, iced gingerbread cookie that has a paleo and lower carb version, with dairy free options."

Serving: 24 | Ready in: 18 m

Ingredients:
- ½ cup coconut flour (sifted, where to buy coconut flour)
- ¼ cup almond flour.
- 1 tsp baking soda.
- cup Sweetener of choice: ½ organic coconut sugar for paleo (or ½ cup erythritol for low carb option.)
- ¾ tsp ground ginger.
- ½ tsp cinnamon.
- 1/8 tsp ground cloves.
- 1/8 tsp cardamom * optional (can omit.)
- 1/8 tsp sea salt.
- 2 eggs (beaten.)
- 1/3 cup butter (melted, or coconut oil, melted, where to buy.)
- 2 tbsp organic molasses.
- Optional Icing:

- 2 tbsp . coconut butter (where to buy coconut butter., or can use 2 tbsp regular butter or coconut oil)
- 2 tbsp unsweetened almond or coconut milk.
- 1/4 tsp lemon juice.
- 1/8 tsp vanilla extract.
- 2 1/2 tsp honey for paleo (or for low carb use 11 drops liquid stevia.)
- Dash ground cinnamon *optional

Direction:

1. Preheat oven to 350 F, and line two baking sheets with parchment paper or grease baking sheets.
2. In a large mixing bowl combine: ½ cup coconut flour, ¼ cup almond flour,
   ½ cup sweetener of choice, 1tsp baking soda, ¾ tsp ground ginger, ½ tsp cinnamon, 1/8 tsp ground cloves, 1/8 tsp optional cardamom, and 1/8 tsp sea salt. Mix together thoroughly.
3. Add to flour mixture in bowl: 2 eggs, 1/3 cup melted butter or coconut oil, and 2 tbsp molasses. Combine thoroughly.
4. The easy way: Form cookie dough into 24 balls, and place on baking sheets. Use a fork to press each ball down a little flatter.
5. The more elaborate way: If you are feeling spunky or have a special occasion, you could put dough between two pieces parchment paper and use a rolling pin to roll out dough and use cookie cutters. use cutters, then peel off top paper. Don't remove cookies from bottom paper, just peel or scrape away excess dough around cookies, and place parchment paper with cookie shapes onto baking sheet (can freeze dough for 10 to 15 mins before rolling if dough is sticky, I didn't but it was cold when I made them).
6. Bake in oven for 10 minutes or until bottoms of cookies are browned.

7. Let cookies cool completely before moving or handling, as they are very fragile until they are cooled off.
8. Now you could make the optional icing if you desire, or serve without icing. They are great either way!
9. In a small sauce pan over medium low heat, warm all icing ingredients until melted. If too thick add more milk of choice. It should be a thick glaze but not a paste (like a glaze texture).
10. Once cookies are cooled, spread a little icing on each cookie. Let icing cool on cookie until icing dries. Could place cookies in fridge to speed up the drying process. Icing will go from liquid to somewhat solid.
11. **Store uneaten cookies in container in fridge.**

Brandy Low Carb Pecan Pie

"What better way to celebrate the festive season than by making a keto pecan pie to take to your gathering with friends? This pie has the perfect pie crust that doesn't crumble all over your shirt and a filling that is not ridiculously sweet. "

Serving: 8 Servings | Ready in: 60 m

Ingredients:

- 1 Cup Almond Flour
- 1/4 Cup Coconut Flour
- 1 Large Egg
- 2 Tbsp Natvia (Or Swerve)
- 1/3 Cup Butter (melted)
- 1 tsp Salt
- 1/4 tsp xanthan gum
- 1 1/2 Cup Pecans (Roughly Chopped)
- 2 Eggs
- 1/4 Cup Natvia (Or Swerve)
- 2 Tbsp Butter (melted)
- 1/4 Cup Brandy (Or Same Amount Sugar Free Maple Syrup)

- 1 tsp Vanilla Extract
- 1 Tbsp Heavy Cream

Direction:
1. Preheat your oven to 180C (355F)
2. Place all of the Pie crust ingreidients into a bowl and mix with an electric mixer until combined
3. Place the filling into a 9" pie pan and press the dough out around the pie pan. Poke small holes into the bottom.
4. Bake in the oven for 10 mins. Cool the pie crust for 1 hour in the fridge (or overnight)
5. Get a large bowl and mix all of the filling with an electric mixer.
6. Place the chopped pecans into the bottom of the pie filling
7. Pour the pie filling into the pie and bake at 180C (355F) for 50 mins.

Nutrition Information:
- Calories: 330 kcal
- Total Fat: 30 g
- Total Carbohydrate: 5 g
- Protein: 6 g

Ketogenic Trifle A Very Keto Christmas

"The keto trifle is a festive treat that is usually the most decadent item on the table. Low and behold, the keto version is a mighty feast."

Serving: 12 People | Ready in: 40 m

Ingredients:

- 1 Cup Ricotta (250g)
- 1/3 Cup Nativa (Or Erythritol)
- 3 Eggs
- 7 Tbsp Butter (melted)
- 3/4 Cup Almond Flour
- 1 tsp baking soda
- 1/2 tsp Salt
- 4 packets sugar-free port wine jelly crystals
- 2 ½ Cups Boiling Water
- 2 Tbps Brandy
- 2 cups Heavy Cream
- 1 cup fresh raspberries
- 1 cup fresh strawberries
- 300 ml thickened cream

Direction:
1. Preheat oven to 160C (340F)
2. Using an electric mixer, beat the ricotta and natvia together.
3. Whilst mixing, add in eggs, 1 at a time.
4. Add melted butter, almond flour, baking soda and salt
5. Pour mixture into a 22cm X 22cm baking tin (9" X 9")
6. Bake for 30 mins.
7. Place jelly crystals in a heatproof bowl. Add boiling water. Stir to dissolve crystals. Stir in 400ml cold water.
8. Refrigerate overnight.
9. Cut the sponge into 2-inch size pieces. Arrange sponge in a 13 cup- capacity serving bowl. Drizzle with brandy.
10. **Spoon half the jelly over top. Top with heavy cream.**
11. **Sprinkle with raspberries and strawberries.**
12. **Spoon remaining jelly over top.**
13. **Refrigerate, covered, overnight.**
14. Using an electric mixer, beat thickened cream and sugar substitute in a bowl until soft peaks form.
15. Spoon mixture over trifle. Top with raspberries and strawberry quarters. Serve.

Nutrition Information:
- Calories: 374 kcal
- Total Fat: 35 g
- Total Carbohydrate: 4 g
- Protein: 6 g

Peanut Butter Chocolate French Silk Pie

Ingredients:

"Macros per slice" Serving: 8 servings | Ready in: 8 m

- 1 cup Anthony's Peanut Flour
- 2 tbsp protein powder
- 2 tbsp erythritol
- 1/2 tsp pink salt
- 1 large egg
- 1 tbsp coconut oil (melted)
- 1/4 cup almond milk
- 3 large eggs
- 2/3 cup erythritol

- 1.5 sticks butter
- 1/4 tsp salt
- 4 oz. unsweetened baker's chocolate (melted)
- 1 tbsp vanilla extract
- 1 cup heavy cream
- 1 tbsp erythritol
- chocolate shavings (optional)

Direction:

1. To make your crust, whisk together your dry ingredients in a mixing bowl.
2. Add your wet ingredients and mix well to combine. You should end up with a sticky dough batter.
3. Press the crust dough into a 9 inch pie pan making sure to press against the sides as well. Pierce the bottom of the crust with a fork (not pictured because we forgot this step!) to prevent bubbling and swelling in the oven. Bake for about 8 minutes in a 350°F oven. It should turn a golden brown. Let it cool completely before filling with chocolate silk batter.
4. To make the chocolate filling, set 3 eggs and 1/3 cup of erythritol onto a double boiler and whisk them together until the erythritol is dissolved and the eggs have thickened. This could take about 5-10 minutes.
5. When your eggs are thick and pale, take them off the heat and allow them to cool while you prep your chocolate.
6. Cream together your butter and another 1/3 cup of erythritol with an electric hand mixer.
7. Add melted chocolate, vanilla extract and salt and beat to combine.
8. To the buttery chocolate mix, add the eggs and stir to combine.
9. Add the chocolate silk batter to your peanut butter crust and refrigerate overnight or for at least 4 hours.

10. When you're ready to serve, whip a cup of heavy whipping cream with a tablespoon of erythritol until it has tripled in volume and stiffened up. Add the whipped cream to the top of the set pie.
11. Serve chilled with chocolate shavings and enjoy!

Nutrition Information:
- Calories: 444 kcal
- Total Fat: 42 g
- Total Carbohydrate: 3.5 g
- Protein: 10 g

Creme de Menthe Cream Puff Tree

"A tower of creme de menthe-flavored puffs makes an eye-catching centerpiece for your dessert table. Guests will have this luscious pyramid deconstructed quickly! Agnes Ward, Stratford, Ontario"

Serving: 60 servings. | Ready in: 01 h 55 m

Ingredients:
- 1-1/4 cups water
- 2/3 cup butter, cubed
- 1-1/4 cups all-purpose flour
- 5 large eggs
- 2 cups heavy whipping cream
- 1/3 cup green creme de menthe
- 1/3 cup butter, cubed
- 2 ounces unsweetened chocolate, chopped
- 2 cups confectioners' sugar
- 1-1/2 teaspoons vanilla extract
- 3 to 6 tablespoons hot water
- Additional confectioners' sugar, optional

Direction:

1. In a large saucepan, bring water and butter to a boil. Add flour all at once and stir until a smooth ball forms. Remove from the heat; let stand

    for 5 minutes. Add eggs, one at a time, beating well after each addition. Continue beating until mixture is smooth and shiny. Drop by rounded teaspoonfuls 2 in. apart onto greased baking sheets., Bake at 400 for 20- 25 minutes or until golden brown. Remove to wire racks.

2. Cut a small slit in the side of each puff to allow steam to escape. Cool puffs., For filling, in a large bowl, beat cream until soft peaks form. Fold in creme de menthe. Pipe about 1 tablespoon into each puff.

3. Refrigerate for up to 2 hours., For glaze, in a small saucepan, combine butter and chocolate. Cook and stir over low heat until melted. Remove from the heat. Using a whisk, stir in the confectioners' sugar, vanilla and enough water to make desired consistency for dipping. Stir until smooth and no lumps appear.,

4. To assemble tree: Separate puffs according to size and shape, choosing the flattest ones for the bottom layer and the smallest ones for the top. Dip the bottoms of the 21 flattest puffs into glaze. Place on a 10-in. round serving platter, in concentric circles forming a solid circle., For the second layer, dip glaze on the bottoms of 15 puffs, then position on base layer.

5. Continue building tree, using about 11 puffs in third layer, about six puffs in fourth layer, about four puffs in fifth layer and one puff on top., Drizzle remaining glaze over tree, thinning with hot water if necessary., Loosely cover tree with plastic wrap and refrigerate for up to 2 hours. Just before serving, dust with confectioners' sugar if desired.

Nutrition Information:
- Calories: 96 calories

- Total Fat: 7g fat (4g saturated fat)
- Cholesterol: 37mg cholesterol
- Sodium: 31mg sodium
- Total Carbohydrate: 7g carbohydrate (4g sugars)
- Protein: 1g protein.
- Fiber: 0 fiber g

Brussels Sprouts Gratin

"This side dish will likely become your family's favorite way to enjoy Brussels sprouts. It's creamy, savory and delicious. Kevin Lieberman, Oklahoma City, Oklahoma"

Serving: 10 servings. | Ready in: 55 m

Ingredients:
- 2 pounds Brussels sprouts, quartered
- 2 tablespoons butter, melted
- 3/4 teaspoon salt
- 1/8 teaspoon pepper
- 1 large onion, chopped
- 3 tablespoons butter
- 3 tablespoons all-purpose flour
- 1 cup whole milk
- 1 cup heavy whipping cream
- 1/8 teaspoon white pepper
- Dash ground nutmeg
- 1/2 cup shredded Gruyere cheese
- 1/4 cup grated Parmesan cheese

Direction:

1. In a large bowl, combine the Brussels sprouts, butter, salt and pepper; toss to coat. Transfer to a greased 13-in. x 9-in. baking dish. Bake,

    uncovered, at 425 for 25-30 minutes or until Brussels sprouts are tender, stirring occasionally., Meanwhile, in a large skillet, saute onion in butter until tender. Stir in flour until blended; gradually add milk and cream. Bring to a boil; cook and stir for 2 minutes or until thickened. Stir in pepper and nutmeg; pour over Brussels sprouts. Sprinkle with cheeses., Reduce heat to 350. Bake, uncovered, for 10-15 minutes or until heated through and cheeses are melted.

Nutrition Information:
- Calories: 233 calories
- Total Fat: 18g fat (11g saturated fat)
- Cholesterol: 58mg cholesterol
- Sodium: 309mg sodium
- Total Carbohydrate: 13g carbohydrate (4g sugars)
- Protein: 7g protein.
- Fiber: 4g fiber

Walnut Filled Pillows

"These tender cookie pillows, filled with a delicious walnut mixture, are my husband's favorite. He says it wouldn't be Christmas without them. Nancy Kostrej, Canonsburg, Pennsylvania"

Serving: 28 cookies. | Ready in: 40 m

Ingredients:
- 1/2 cup cold butter, cubed
- 3 ounces cold cream cheese
- 1-1/4 cups all-purpose flour
- 3/4 cup ground walnuts
- 1/4 cup sugar
- 2 tablespoons whole milk
- 1/2 teaspoon vanilla or almond extract
- 1 large egg, lightly beaten
- Confectioners' sugar

Direction:

1. In a large bowl, cut butter and cream cheese into flour until mixture resembles coarse crumbs. Blend mixture together until smooth dough forms, about 3 minutes. Pat into a rectangle; wrap in plastic. Refrigerate for 1 hour or until firm. For filling, combine the walnuts, sugar, milk and vanilla., Unwrap dough and place on a lightly floured surface.
2. Roll into a 17-1/2x10-in. rectangle; cut into 2-1/2-in. squares. Place a level teaspoonful of filling in the center of each square. Moisten edges with water; fold in half and seal with a fork. Place 1 in. apart on ungreased baking sheets. Brush with egg., Bake at 375 for 10-12 minutes or until edges are golden brown. Remove to wire racks to cool.
3. Dust with confectioners' sugar.

Nutrition Information:
- Calories: 84 calories
- Total Fat: 6g fat (3g saturated fat)
- Cholesterol: 20mg cholesterol
- Sodium: 45mg sodium
- Total Carbohydrate: 6g carbohydrate (2g sugars)
- Protein: 1g protein.
- Fiber: 0 fiber g

Almond Joy Cookies Low Carb Sugar Free Thms

"With only 4 Ingredients, these are my FAVORITE low carb cookie!" Serving: 16 cookies | Ready in: 30 m

Ingredients:
- 1 1/2 Cups Unsweetened Shredded Coconut (you want the finely shredded, not the large flakes)
- 1/2 Cup Sliced Almonds
- 1 Cup Lily's Stevia Sweetened Chocolate Chips
- 1 Cup 3 Ingredient Low Carb Sugar Free Sweetened Condensed Milk

Direction:
4. Preheat oven to 325.
1. Make Sweetened Condensed Milk and allow to cool completely.

2. Mix unsweetened coconut, almonds, and chocolate chips.
3. Add Sweetened Condensed Milk to coconut mixture and stir until combined.
4. Using a small cookie scoop, place "dough" in the cavities of a greased muffin tin.
5. With your fingers, press cookies down slightly.
6. Bake for 15 minutes, or until edges are turning golden brown.
7. Remove from oven and place the muffin tin in the freezer for 30 minutes. (The cookies are very soft when they come out of the oven. Placing them in the freezer helps them firm up so they are not crumbly.)
8. akes approximately 16 cookies.
9. Store leftovers in the refrigerator or freezer.

Nutrition Information:
- Calories: 237 kcal
- Total Fat: 40.5 g
- Saturated Fat: 16.5 g
- Cholesterol: 29 mg
- Sodium: 18 mg
- Total Carbohydrate: 6 g
- Protein: 12.5 g
- Fiber: 4 g
- Sugar: 3 g

Baklava Cookies Low Carb Gluten Free

"These Baklava Cookies are an easy and healthy alternative to the traditional layered pastry."

Serving: 24 cookies | Ready in: 50 m

Ingredients:

- 3 oz cream cheese (softened)
- 1 4 oz stick butter (softened)
- 1/3 cup almond flour
- 1/3 cup coconut flour
- 1/3 cup ground golden flax
- ¾ cup chopped nuts (I used ½ cup walnuts and ¼ cup pistachios)
- ½ tsp cinnamon
- ½ cup Trim Healthy Mama Gentle Sweet (or my sweetener)
- 1 tbsp water
- 3 one inch pieces of lemon zest
- 1 cinnamon stick
- 3 tsp honey (optional, see note below)

Direction:

1. Preheat oven to 350. Spray a mini muffin tin with cooking spray.

2. Mix the dough ingredients in a medium bowl with a wooden spoon. If the butter and cream cheese is room temperature they mix easily. Divide into 24 pieces and press into the holes of a mini muffin tin. Use a tart tamper, an upside down measuring teaspoon, or your fingers.
3. Combine the nuts and cinnamon. Divide between the prepared mini muffin tin. Bake for 20-22 minutes until the dough is golden. Cool to room temperature.
4. Meanwhile, make the syrup. Combine the sweetener, water, lemon zest, and cinnamon stick in a small saucepan. Cook over medium low until it simmers. Reduce heat to low and simmer for 5 minutes. Cool to room temperature.
5. Drizzle the syrup over the cookie cups. If using the honey spoon 1/8 of a tsp over each. Remove from the muffin tin and enjoy!

Nutrition Information:
- Calories: 109 kcal
- Total Fat: 10 g
- Saturated Fat: 2 g
- Cholesterol: 3 mg
- Sodium: 54 mg
- Total Carbohydrate: 3 g
- Protein: 1 g
- Fiber: 1 g
- Sugar: 1 g

Easy Sugarfree Oatmeal Cookies Low Carb Glutenfree

"This gluten-free & sugar-free oatmeal cookies recipe creates the perfect moist, low carb cookie. Only 9 ingredients, 4 grams net carbs, and ready in 20 minutes!"

Serving: 22 2.5" cookies | Ready in: 20 m

Ingredients:

- 1 1/4 cup Gluten-free rolled oats (Bob's Red Mill)
- 1 1/4 cup Blanched almond flour
- 1 tsp Gluten-free baking powder
- 1 tsp Cinnamon
- 1/4 tsp Sea salt
- 1/2 cup Butter (preferably grass-fed, softened)
- 2 large Egg
- 3/4 cup Erythritol
- 1 tsp Vanilla extract

Direction:

1. Preheat the oven to 350 degrees F (177 degrees C). Line a cookie sheet with parchment paper or a silicone mat.

2. In a large bowl, stir together the gluten-free rolled oats, almond flour, baking powder, cinnamon, and sea salt.
3. Combine the butter, eggs, vanilla extract, and erythritol in a blender. Puree until fluffy.
4. Stir the wet mixture from the blender into the dry mixture, until just combined. (Add a small amount of water to thin out the batter if it's dry; it should be pliable but not crumbly.)
5. Scoop rounded tablespoonfuls of batter onto the lined cookie sheet, approximately two inches apart. (Leaving space around them is important - they will spread.) Flatten slightly with your hands to about 1/4 to 1/3 in (.6-.8 cm) thickness.
6. Bake 11-16 minutes, until cookies are barely set and edges are golden (less time for chewy cookies, more for crispy). Cool completely before moving.

Nutrition Information:
- Calories: 103 kcal
- Total Fat: 8 g
- Saturated Fat: 3 g
- Cholesterol: 31 mg
- Sodium: 36 mg
- Total Carbohydrate: 5 g
- Protein: 3 g
- Fiber: 1 g
- Sugar: 0.4 g

Iced Lemon Cookies Low Carb Grain Sugar Free THM S

Serving: 2 dozen cookies | Ready in: 23 m

Ingredients:

- 1 stick cold salted butter (cut into pieces)
- 1 cup almond flour
- 1/3 cup coconut flour
- 1/3 cup Trim Healthy Mama Gentle Sweet (or my sweetener blend)
- 2 tsp gelatin
- 1 tsp lemon extract
- 1 cup powdered sweetener that measures 1:1 for sugar (such as sukrin or swerve)
- 1-2 tbsp lemon juice
- lemon zest (optional)

Direction:

1. Preheat oven to 350.
2. Next, combine all the dough ingredients in the food processor and pulse until a uniform dough forms. Divide into 24 balls and put on a parchment-lined baking sheet. Press down with your fingers. Sprinkle with a little more sweetener.

3. Bake for 12-15 minutes or until lightly browned around the edges. Cool for at least 10 minutes.
4. Combine the powdered sweetener with 1 tablespoon lemon juice in a small bowl. Stir until smooth. Add additional lemon juice if needed. Spread on the cooled cookies.
5. Garnish with lemon zest.

Low Carb Almond Flour Cookies Recipe GlutenFree Shortbread Cookies 4 Ingredients

"This buttery, low carb almond flour cookies recipe has 4 ingredients & 1g net carbs each! Keto gluten-free shortbread cookies with almond flour taste like real ones."

Serving: 18 2-1/4" cookies | Ready in: 22 m

Ingredients:
- 2 1/2 cups Blanched almond flour
- 6 tbsp Butter ((softened; can use coconut oil for dairy-free, but flavor and texture will be different) *)
- 1/2 cup Erythritol ((or other granular sweetener of choice)**)
- 1 tsp Vanilla extract

Direction:
1. Preheat the oven to 350 degrees F (177 degrees C). Line a cookie sheet with parchment paper.
2. Use a hand mixer or stand mixer to beat together the butter and erythritol, until it's fluffy and light in color.
3. Beat in the vanilla extract. Beat in the almond flour, 1/2 cup (64 g) at a time. (The dough will be dense and a little crumbly, but should stick when pressed together.)

4. Scoop rounded tablespoonfuls of the dough onto the prepared cookie sheet. Flatten each cookie to about 1/3 in (.8 cm) thick. (You can make them thicker or thinner to your liking. Keep in mind they will not spread or thin out during baking, so make them as thin as you want them when done.)
5. Bake for about 12 minutes, until the edges are golden. Allow to cool completely in the pan before handling (cookies will harden as they cool).

Nutrition Information:
- Calories: 124 kcal
- Total Fat: 12 g
- Saturated Fat: 3 g
- Cholesterol: 10 mg
- Sodium: 6 mg
- Total Carbohydrate: 3.3 g
- Protein: 3 g
- Fiber: 1.6 g
- Sugar: 1 g

Sugarfree Gingerbread Cookies Low Carb Paleo

"This sugar-free gingerbread cookies recipe uses just 5 ingredients plus a few spices. It's also low carb, paleo, and gluten-free."

Serving: 10 large 4.5" cookies | Ready in: 25 m

Ingredients:
- 2 cups Blanched almond flour
- 1 tbsp Cinnamon
- 1 1/2 tsp Ground ginger
- 1/4 tsp Ground cloves
- 1/4 tsp Nutmeg
- 1/2 tsp Gluten-free baking powder
- 1/4 cup Erythritol
- 1/4 cup Butter (softened)
- 1 large Egg
- 1 tsp Vanilla extract

Direction:
1. In a medium bowl, stir together the almond flour, cinnamon, ground ginger, ground cloves, nutmeg, and baking powder.

2. In a large bowl, use a hand mixer to beat the butter and erythritol for 1-2 minutes, until fluffy. Beat in the egg and vanilla extract. Beat in the almond flour mixture until a dough forms.
3. Form the dough into a ball and refrigerate for at least 30 minutes, or until ready to bake.
4. Preheat the to 350 degrees F (177 degrees C). Line a cookie sheet with parchment paper (you may need to do this twice for all the cookies).
5. Place the ball of dough between two large pieces of parchment paper. Roll out to 1/4 in (.6 cm) thickness. Use a cookie cutter to cut out cookie shapes and transfer them to the parchment paper. (Transferring can be tricky because the dough is very soft. You can use a thin turner or flat spatula to help transfer each one.) When you've cut out all the shapes you can, re-form the remaining dough into a ball, roll it out again, and repeat, until you've used up all the dough.
6. Bake for 10-15 minutes, until golden on the edges. Cool on the cookie sheet before handling.

Nutrition Information:
- Calories: 180 kcal
- Total Fat: 16 g
- Saturated Fat: 4 g
- Cholesterol: 34 mg
- Sodium: 16 mg
- Total Carbohydrate: 6 g
- Protein: 6 g
- Fiber: 3 g
- Sugar: 1 g

Tagalong Peanut Butter Cookie Bars

"Tagalong Cookies simplified to just 6 ingredients & ready in an hour! These chocolate peanut butter cookie bars taste like your favorite Girl Scout treat! Keto, Low Carb, THM, Grain-Free, Sugar-Free, Gluten-Free."

Serving: 16 bars | Ready in: 60 m

Ingredients:
- 3/4 cups almond flour
- 3 tbsp Trim Healthy Mama Gentle Sweet (or my sweetener)
- pinch of salt
- 3 tbsp butter (softened)
- 1 tsp vanilla
- 1/2 cup peanut butter
- 3 tbsp Trim Healthy Mama Gentle Sweet (or my sweetener)
- 1/2 tsp vanilla
- 3.5 oz 85% dark chocolate or sugar free chocolate (chopped)

Direction:
1. Preheat oven to 350.

2. In a medium bowl mix all the shortbread ingredients until combined. Press into the bottom of a square 8x8 baking dish.
3. Bake for 15-20 minutes or until golden brown.
4. Meanwhile, combine the peanut butter ingredients. If your peanut butter is cold you can microwave it for 30 seconds to soften it.
5. When the shortbread comes out of the oven drop little blobs of the peanut on top of it. Spread gently with a spatula. The heat from the cookie will help spread the peanut butter. Be gentle or the bottom layer can crumble.
6. Melt the chocolate in the microwave or double boiler. Pour over the peanut butter. Spread gently. Put in the refrigerator until firm. Cut into squares and enjoy!

Nutrition Information:
- Calories: 128 kcal
- Total Fat: 12 g
- Saturated Fat: 4 g
- Cholesterol: 5 mg
- Sodium: 57 mg
- Total Carbohydrate: 4 g
- Protein: 3 g
- Fiber: 2 g
- Sugar: 1 g

Cranberry Ginger Butter Cookies Low Carb and Gluten Free

"Low carb butter Cookies chock full of sugar-free dried cranberries and sugar-free crystallized ginger. Perfect as a holiday treat or anytime!"

Serving: 32 small cookies | Ready in: 33 m

Ingredients:
- 2 cups almond flour
- 1 tsp baking powder
- ¼ tsp salt
- ½ cup butter (softened)
- ¾ cup Swerve Sweetener (or granulated erythritol)
- 1 large egg
- ½ cup sugar-free dried cranberries (chopped)
- ¼ cup chopped sugar-free candied ginger (chopped)

Direction:
1. Preheat oven to 325 F and line a baking sheet with parchment paper.
2. In a medium bowl, whisk together almond flour, baking powder and salt.

3. In a large bowl, beat butter with Swerve until light and fluffy, about 2 minutes. Beat in egg, then beat in almond flour mixture until well combined.
4. Stir in chopped cranberries and ginger.
5. Form into ¾ inch balls and place 1 inch apart on prepared cookie sheet (You may find you need two sheets, depending on size).
6. Take a flat-bottomed glass and cover with parchment paper. Secure parchment with a rubber band. Press cookies to ¼ inch thick.
7. Bake 11 to 13 minutes, or until edges are beginning to brown. Remove from oven and let cool on pan 5 minutes, then carefully transfer to a wire rack to cool completely.

Nutrition Information:
- Total Carbohydrate: 4.8 g
- Fiber: 2 g

3-Ingredient Chocolate Mousse Low Carb

"Rich Chocolate Mousse in minutes! No eggs. No dairy. And only 3 ingredients to thick, creamy and rich chocolate mousse that happens to be low carb and real really good for you. Weight Watchers: 5pp per serve (out of 8 serves)"

Serving: 8 people | Ready in: 5 m

Ingredients:

- 2 x 400ml ((13.7oz) cans full fat coconut cream or coconut milk)
- 2 tablespoons confectioners sweetener (or confectioners | icing sugar if not counting carbs)
- 3 tablespoons unsweetened cocoa powder
- pinch of salt (optional! About 1/4 teaspoon. Adjust to your tastes)
- 20 g | 2 squares 70% chocolate (shaved (optional for extra richness -- or sugar free chocolate chips)
- extra shaved chocolate to garnish

Direction:

1. Place sealed cans of coconut cream (or milk) in the refrigerator overnight. Without shaking the cans, open carefully and scoop out the thick cream sitting at the top

above the water. Transfer the thick hard cream to a bowl and discard all of the liquid left in the bottom of the cans (or reserve to add into smoothies later).
2. Add the sweetener (or sugar if using) and beat on high using a hand mixer (or whisk) until thick and creamy (about 1-2 minutes). Reserve about 4 tablespoons of the plain 'whipped cream' to use as a topping to serve with and set aside.
3. Fold the cocoa powder and salt through the cream and beat (or whisk) again until smooth, well combined and thick. Fold through the shaved chocolate if using). Depending on the coconut milk you use, a mousse will form almost immediately once the cocoa powder is mixed through. If not, refrigerate until set and ready to serve, or serve immediately. Dollop the 'plain whipped cream' over the mousse and sprinkle with shaved chocolate (if using).

Nutrition Information:
- Calories: 334 kcal
- Total Fat: 31 g
- Saturated Fat: 28 g
- Sodium: 4 mg
- Total Carbohydrate: 5 g
- Protein: 3 g
- Fiber: 2 g

Chocolate Champagne Cupcakes with Raspberry Icing

Serving: 20 cupcakes | Ready in: 75 m

Ingredients:
- 1/2 cup Honeyville unsweetened Dutch-process cocoa powder
- 1/4 cup hot water
- 1.5 cups Honeyville blanched almond flour
- 1 tsp baking powder
- 1.5 sticks (6 oz butter, softened)
- 1 cup sugar free sweetener (I use my blend of xylitol, erythritol, and stevia)
- 2 large eggs (room temperature)
- 1 tsp vanilla
- 1/2 cup sour cream (room temperature)
- 1 1/3 cups frozen raspberries
- 1/4 cup sugar free sweetener (I use my blend of xylitol, erythritol, and stevia)
- 3 tbsp champagne
- 1/2 tsp gluccomannan
- 1 stick butter (softened)

- 6 oz cream cheese (softened)
- 1 cup sugar free sweetener (I use my blend of xylitol, erythritol, and stevia, finely ground)
- 2/3 cup frozen raspberries (thawed)
- 2 tbsp champagne

Direction:

1. Preheat oven to 350. Line 20 cupcake holes with liners.
2. Combine all the ingredients for the cupcakes in a large bowl and beat with an electric mixer until smooth. Divide between the prepared cupcake tins. Bake for 30 minutes. Cool completely. They will sink a bit creating a well for the filling.
3. Meanwhile, combine the first 3 filling ingredients in a small saucepan over medium-low heat and simmer for 5 minutes. Sprinkle the gluccomannan on top and stir well. Set aside.
4. Next, to make the icing, beat the cream cheese and butter until smooth with an electric mixer. Beat in the sweetener, raspberries, and champagne.
5. When the cupcakes have cooled divide the filling between them. Pipe the icing on top. Store in the refrigerator.

Chocolate Fudge Keto Cookies

Serving: 10 Cookies | Ready in: 25 m

Ingredients:
- 1/2 cup swerve confectioner
- 1/2 cup Unsweetened Cocoa Powder
- 4 tbsp Butter
- 2 large Egg
- 1 tsp vanilla extract
- 1 cup Almond Flour
- 1 tsp Baking powder
- 1 pinch Pink Salt

Direction:
1. Combine cocoa powder and swerve confectioners sugar in a mixing bowl.
2. Add melted butter to mixture and combine with a hand mixer.
3. Once combined, add eggs, vanilla, and baking powder and mix again.
4. Now add the almond flour and mix one last time. You should have a fairly thick batter that can easily be shaped by hand.

5. Form into cookies and place on a greased baking sheet. The cookies will remain the shape you form them to after cooking. They do not expand too much.
6. Dust the tops of cookies with erythritol. (optional)
7. Bake at 350 for 12-15 minutes. Let cool and enjoy! These are great straight out of the freezer as well. These can be frozen for 2-3 months!

Nutrition Information:
- Calories: 132 kcal
- Total Fat: 11.6 g
- Total Carbohydrate: 4.8 g
- Protein: 4.4 g
- Fiber: 2.8 g

Kentucky Butter Cake

"This gorgeous indulgent low carb Kentucky Butter Cake is going to blow your mind! It's easily one of the best keto cake recipes I have ever made."

Serving: 16 | Ready in: 80 m

Ingredients:

- 2 1/2 cups almond flour
- 1/4 cup coconut flour
- 1/4 cup unflavoured whey protein powder
- 1 tbsp baking powder
- 1/2 tsp salt
- 1 cup butter (softened)
- 1 cup Swerve Granular
- 5 large eggs (room temperature.)
- 2 tsp vanilla extract
- 1/2 cup whipping cream
- 1/2 cup water
- 5 tbsp butter
- 1/3 cup Swerve Granular
- 2 tbsp water
- 1 tsp vanilla extract
- 1 to 2 tbsp Confectioner's Swerve

Direction:

1. Preheat oven to 325F. Grease a bundt cake pan VERY well and then dust with a few tbsp of almond flour.
2. In a medium bowl, whisk together the almond flour, coconut flour, whey protein, baking powder, and salt.
3. In a large bowl, beat the butter and the sweetener together until light and creamy. Beat in the eggs and vanilla extract.

Beat in the almond flour mixture and then beat in the whipping cream and water until well combined.

4. Transfer the batter to the prepared baking pan and smooth the top. Bake 50 to 60 minutes, until golden brown and the cake is firm to the touch. A tester inserted in the center should come out clean.
5. Butter Glaze:In a small saucepan over low heat, melt the butter and sweetener together. Whisk until well combined. Whisk in the water and vanilla extract.
6. While the cake is still warm and in the pan, poke holes all over with a skewer. Pour the glaze over and let cool completely in the pan.
7. Gently loosen the sides with a knife or thin rubber spatula, then flip out onto a serving platter. Dust with powdered sweetener.
8. Serve with lightly sweetened whipped cream and fresh berries.

Nutrition Information:
- Calories: 301 kcal
- Total Fat: 27.07 g
- Cholesterol: 109 mg
- Total Carbohydrate: 5.54 g
- Protein: 7.34 g
- Fiber: 2.5 g

Keto Chocolate Salami

"Looking for something moreish to take along to a Xmas party? Look no further as this keto chocolate salami is a hit with everyone and easy to make ahead."

Serving: 30 | Ready in: 30 m

Ingredients:

- 200 g 85% Dark Chocolate, chopped (7 oz)
- 125 g Butter, softened (4.4 oz)
- 1/2 cup Powdered Sweetener
- 1 tsp Vanilla
- 1 Egg, large
- 1 cup Keto Nut & Seed Granola
- 70 g Pork Rinds/Crackle Chips, crushed lightly (2.4 oz)

Direction:

1. Melt the chocolate in a glass bowl over a pan of simmering water. Set aside to cool.
2. Beat the butter, sweetener and vanilla on high speed until pale and fluffy.
3. Add the egg and beat on low speed until combined. It may appear to split, but don't panic it will come together.

4. Add the cooled chocolate to the butter mixture and stir to combine until completely smooth.
5. Add the pork rinds and granola and stir to combine. Set aside to slightly harden so you can shape and roll the mixture
6. Shape the mixture into a log approximately 30cms long on a sheet of glad wrap. Wrap tightly and twist the ends of the glad wrap (like a bon bon) to tighten and smooth the sides. Refrigerate overnight to set.
7. To serve, remove from the glad wrap. Dust with powdered sweetener and and slice into 1 cm rounds.

Nutrition Information:
- Calories: 107 kcal
- Total Fat: 9 g
- Saturated Fat: 4 g
- Cholesterol: 16 mg
- Sodium: 74 mg
- Total Carbohydrate: 2 g
- Protein: 2 g

Lava Cake for 1 Low Carb

"Lava Cake for 1 makes warm, sweet, chocolaty gooey goodness in minutes. With just over 2 net carbs it is a very satisfying low carb treat. Great for Keto and gluten free."

Serving: 1 cake | Ready in: 18 m

Ingredients:
- 2 T . Almond flour
- 1 T . unsweetened cocoa powder
- 2 T . Swerve granular Sweetener
- tiny pinch salt
- 1/8 th tsp. vanilla
- 1 T . butter (softened)
- 1 large egg (beaten)

Direction:
1. Heat oven to 350 degrees.
2. Grease a ramekin or mist with vegetable oil spray.
3. Stir together the dry ingredients in a small bowl.

4. Add the wet ingredients and stir together until thoroughly mixed and pour into prepared ramekin.
5. Bake for 12-15 minutes until top is set.
6. Allow to cool slightly before serving.

Nutrition Information:
- Calories: 257 kcal

Low Carb Christmas Pudding

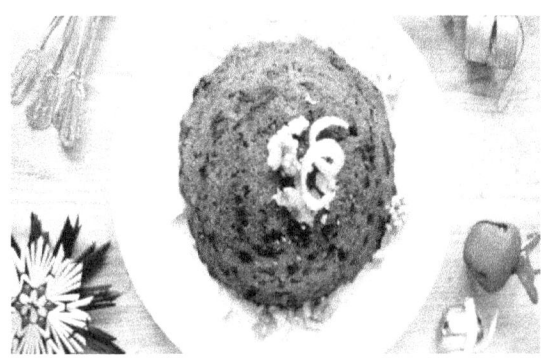

"Enjoy this low carb Christmas pudding as the crowning glory of your festive meal. It's sugar free, gluten free and suitable for diabetics. Even better, it's ready in just over 10 minutes!"

Serving: 4 portions | Ready in: 1 m

Ingredients:

- 100 g / 1 cup almond flour
- 1 egg
- 100 g / 1/2 cup shredded carrot
- 50 g / 1/4 cup blueberries, frozen
- 50 g / 1/4 cup cherries (frozen)
- 10 g small handful crushed walnuts
- 2 tbsp butter (melted)
- 1 tbsp double (heavy cream)
- 1 tsp baking powder
- 1 tsp cacao powder (unsweetened)
- 2 tbsp powdered sweetener (or more to taste)
- 2 tsp mixed spice (pumpkin spice)

- 2 tsp cinnamon
- orange zest from 1/2 orange
- optional: glug of brandy
- double (heavy cream, to serve)

Direction:

1. Blitz the carrot in a food processor or grate them. Add the fruit (I used frozen blueberries and cherries) and chop. Your chopped carrots and fruit combined should fill 1 US measuring cup.
2. Mix the dry ingredients in a bowl.
3. Melt the butter.
4. Add the melted butter and all remaining ingredients to the bowl and stir until combined. If you wish, add a glug of Brandy. Adjust sweetener if needed.
5. Grease a pyrex glass bowl with butter and fill in the Christmas pudding batter. Microwave at 700W for 6 minutes.
6. Turn out upside down onto a plate and serve with thick cream.

Nutrition Information:
- Calories: 271 kcal
- Total Fat: 22 g
- Cholesterol: 59 mg
- Sodium: 36 mg
- Total Carbohydrate: 12.5 g
- Protein: 8.4 g
- Fiber: 4.5 g
- Sugar: 5.2 g

Maple Macadamia Nut Cookies

Serving: 20 Cookies | Ready in: 10 m

Ingredients:

- 2 cups Almond Flour
- 1/4 cup macadamia nuts
- 5 tbsp erythritol
- 2 tbsp Butter
- 1 large Egg
- 2 tsp vanilla extract
- 1/4 cup sugar free maple syrup
- 1/2 tsp Baking Soda

Direction:

1. Using hand mixer combine room temperature butter and erythritol.
2. Add egg, vanilla, baking soda, and maple syrup and mix until combined well.
3. Slowly add the almond flour as you mix. Once you have formed a dough fold in the macadamia nuts.
4. Don't worry, the dough will be sticky.

5. Place balls of dough onto a greased baking sheet and flatten out to desired cookie size.
6. Bake in 350 degree oven for 12 minutes.
7. Allow to cool for at least 20 minutes. Enjoy!

Nutrition Information:
- Calories: 85 kcal
- Total Fat: 7.75 g
- Total Carbohydrate: 2.6 g
- Protein: 2.5 g
- Fiber: 1.2 g

Sour Cream Cake

"An incredibly moist low carb sheet cake topped with whipped cream cheese frosting and decorated with fresh berries. This Sour Cream Cake is perfect for July 4th and all summer."

Serving: 12 | Ready in: 50 m

Ingredients:

- 3 cups almond flour (280 g)
- 2/3 cup Sukrin :1 (See menu bar for gram conversion)
- 1 tsp sea salt
- 1/2 tsp baking soda
- 3 large eggs (I always use cold)
- 1/2 cup sour cream
- 1/4 cup salted butter, melted (4 tbsp, 2 oz)
- 2 tsp vanilla extract
- 1/2 tsp stevia glycerite
- 6 oz cold cream cheese
- 1/3 cup Sukrin Icing Sugar
- 1/4 cup salted butter (very soft) (4 tbps, 2 oz)

- 3/4 cup heavy cream
- 1 tsp vanilla extract
- 1/4 tsp stevia glycerite (or to taste)
- 6 medium strawberries, halved
- 36 small blueberries
- 12 mint sprigs (optional)

Direction:
1. Preheat oven to 325 F. Generously butter and flour a 10-inch Bundt cake pan.
2. Into a bowl, sift together the flour, baking powder, and salt; set aside.
3. In a mixing bowl with an electric mixer, cream 1 cup butter with the granulated sugar; beat at high speed until mixture is very light and fluffy, about 5 minutes.
4. Beat in the eggs, one at a time, beating well after each addition and scraping down the side of bowl frequently.
5. Blend in lemon zest.
6. Add flour mixture to the creamed mixture alternately with sour cream, ending with the dry ingredients. Scrape sides of bowl frequently.
7. Pour batter into prepared cake pan; bake in the preheated oven for 55 to 65 minutes, or until a cake tester or wooden pick inserted near the center of the cake comes out clean.
8. Cool in pan 10 minutes.
9. Meanwhile, combine lemon glaze ingredients in a bowl, blending until smooth.
10. **Carefully turn the lemon cake out onto a platter; drizzle evenly with glaze.**

Nutrition Information:
- Calories: 358 kcal
- Total Fat: 34.5 g
- Cholesterol: 121 mg

- Sodium: 362 mg
- Total Carbohydrate: 7 g
- Protein: 8.6 g
- Fiber: 2.5 g

Cream Cheese Cookies Gluten Free

"Yummy low carb cookies made with cream cheese. These tasty sugar free cookies can be pressed or cut into festive shapes for any holiday."

Serving: 18 people | Ready in: 22 m

Ingredients:
- 1 cup butter
- 3/4 cup low carb sweetener (or other sugar substitute)
- 4 ounces cream cheese (softened)
- 1 egg
- 2 cups almond flour
- 1/2 cup coconut flour
- 1 teaspoon vanilla extract (see note)

Direction:
1. Cream the butter and sweetener until light and fluffy.
2. Beat in the cream cheese.
3. Add in the egg.
4. Stir in the the flours, then mix in the vanilla.

5. Chill dough for at least 4 hours.
6. Squeeze dough out of cookie press or roll out into a cookie log and slice.
7. Bake at 350F until cookies begin to brown (about 8-10 minutes for pressed cookie or 10-12 minutes for slices). Cook longer for crisper cookies.

Nutrition Information:
- Calories: 200 kcal
- Total Fat: 19 g
- Saturated Fat: 8 g
- Cholesterol: 43 mg
- Sodium: 120 mg
- Total Carbohydrate: 4 g
- Protein: 3 g
- Fiber: 2 g

Gluten Free Thumbprint Cookies with Jam

"Here's a subtly sweet shortbread cookie with a dollop of raspberry jam on top. It's a gluten free cookie you'll want to make year round."

Serving: 36 cookies | Ready in: 30 m

Ingredients:

- 1/2 cup coconut oil (liquified)
- 1/2 cup butter (melted)
- 3 tablespoons Pyure All Purpose (or 6 tablespoons Swerve)
- 2 egg yolks
- 1 teaspoon sugar free vanilla extract
- 2/3 cup coconut flour
- 1 1/3 cup almond flour (fine ground)
- 1 teaspoon xanthan gum
- 1 batch of chia raspberry jam

Direction:

1. Preheat oven to 350°F. Line cookie sheet with parchment paper or silicone mat.
2. In large bowl, beat together coconut oil, butter, sweetener, yolks, and vanilla.

3. Beat in coconut and almond flours (and optional xanthan gum) until dough forms.
4. Scoop dough balls evenly onto lined cookie sheet.
5. Use the tip of a finger to create an indentation on the top of each cookie.
6. Fill each cookie indentation with chia raspberry jam.
7. Bake at 350°F for 12 to 15 minutes.

Nutrition Information:
- Calories: 85 kcal
- Total Fat: 8.3 g
- Sodium: 23.1 mg
- Total Carbohydrate: 5 g
- Fiber: 2.1 g

Grainfree Spice Cookies Autoimmune Paleo Vegan

Serving: 30 small cookies

Ingredients:
- 1 cup organic coconut butter (240 g; softened)
- 3 Tbsp honey
- 1 tsp ground cloves (freshly ground; may need more if not freshly ground)
- 1 Tbsp organic cinnamon
- 2 tsp organic ginger
- 1/4 tsp salt
- 1/2 tsp baking soda
- 1 Tbsp organic coconut oil
- 1 Tbsp gelatin powder
- 7 tsp water (divided)

Direction:
1. Preheat oven to 350° F/180° C.
2. Sprinkle gelatin powder over 2 Tbsp of cold water in a tiny pot (for stovetop) or bowl (for microwave) and let soften.

3. Mix together softened coconut butter, honey, spices, salt, and baking soda in a larger bowl.
4. Add coconut oil to the gelatin/water mix and warm up, on the stove top or in a microwave until everything has melted. Watch it like a hawk - it burns quickly. I don't have a microwave, so I couldn't tell you how long to mix it for.
5. Pour the gelatin mixture over the coconut mixture and immediately mix. At this point it is very crumbly, it doesn't stick together like normal cookie dough at all. Add the last tsp of cold water.
6. This is the way I shaped them: place a tablespoon of 'dough' in one hand and squeeze, like you're going to make a ball. It will start to stick together. With your other hand, make a circle with your thumb and pointer finger. Put the 'dough' in the circle and press it together with the other hand's thumb and pointer finger, until it has filled the circle and sticks together.
7. Place on a greased cookie sheet and bake for 7-10 min, until lightly golden. Shorter baking times will give a more moist cookie, longer baking will render a drier cookie. As the cookies don't spread, you can place them fairly close together.
8. Eat, enjoy, and decide that AIP can be pretty good.

No Bake Coconut Cookies Coconut Delights sugar dairy egg and grain free

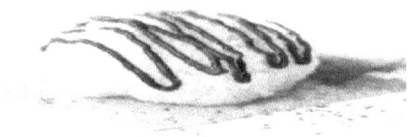

"These vegan No Bake Coconut Cookies come together super quick and are loaded with healthy ingredients. Plus they're paleo and sugar-free too!"

Serving: 8 | Ready in: 5 m

Ingredients:
- 3 cups organic unsweetened shredded coconut
- 3/8 cup organic coconut oil
- 1/2 cup xylitol
- 2 tsp vanilla
- 3/8 tsp salt
- Homemade Chocolate / Carob Chips ((melted for drizzle))
- coconut shreds
- finely-chopped nuts

Direction:
1. Put all ingredients in a food processor or blender.
2. Combine until the mixture is blended and sticks together. (Note: if you are using a high-powered blender like a Vitamix, do not turn your machine on high. You will likely

end up with Coconut Butter. While it will be delicious, it won't be these no-bake cookies.
3. Remove the mixture from the blender / food processor and form into desired shape. I really like the cute little shapes I was able to make with this little cookie scoop. I had a little trouble with the "balls" falling apart but just gently press them back into the desired shape.
4. Decorate with shredded coconut, cocoa or carob powder, crushed nuts, or melted chocolate (I used my Homemade Chocolate OR Carob Chips, piped from a plastic baggie with a tiny hole cut in the corner) as desired. Or leave them plain. They are great just as is (but I do think a little coconut sprinkled on top adds a nice touch.
5. Leave to firm up on a plate. They will firm up at room temperature.
6. You really don't need to store these in the fridge but I think they taste a tad bit better cold.

Nutrition Information:
- Total Fat: 34.2 g
- Saturated Fat: 29.8 g
- Sodium: 124 mg
- Total Carbohydrate: 21.1 g
- Protein: 3 g
- Fiber: 6 g
- Sugar: 3.1 g

Pumpkin Snicker doodles gluten dairy sugar free w vegan grain free options

"These Pumpkin Snicker doodles are gluten free and sugar free with egg and dairy-free options. They're our "go to" cookies recipe whenever it's baking time!"

Serving: 19 cookies

Ingredients:
- 1/2 cup organic coconut oil ((or healthy fat alternative like butter))
- 3/4 cup xylitol
- 1 large egg or equivalent substitute
- 1/2 cup organic pumpkin puree
- 1/2 tsp organic pure vanilla extract
- 2 cups flour (whole grain preferred)
- 1 tsp organic cinnamon
- 1/2 tsp organic nutmeg
- 1/2 tsp organic ground ginger
- 3/4 tsp baking soda
- 1/2 tsp salt
- 1/2 cup granulated sweetener ((as healthy as possible))

- 1 tsp organic cinnamon
- 1/4 tsp organic nutmeg

Direction:

1. Preheat oven to 350 degrees Fahrenheit.

2. Combine ingredients for Cinnamon Coating and set aside for later use.

3. Combine flour, salt, baking soda and spices in a medium-sized bowl.

4. If coconut oil is not soft enough to mix easily, melt in a pan over low heat. Place in a bowl.

5. Add sweetener and egg (or substitute) to the softened oil. Beat well. Add pumpkin puree and vanilla. Beat well again.

6. Add dry ingredients to wet ingredients. Mix thoroughly, but do not over- mix.

7. Take a small amount of dough (I use a small cookie scoop for this process), roll into balls, drop in cinnamon sugar topping, and roll to coat. (NOTE: For gluten-free cookies, the smaller the cookie the better as they will crumble more easily than those made with gluten flours.)

8. Place on a baking stone or cookie sheet (I highly recommend baking stones) about 2 inches apart, flattening a bit with your hand (or the bottom of a glass).

9. Bake for about 10 minutes, or until slightly golden brown.

10. Cool for approximately 5 minutes before removing from baking sheet to cool on a cooling rack.

11. **Try not to eat them all at once .**

Nutrition Information:
- Total Fat: 11.7 g
- Saturated Fat: 9.7 g
- Cholesterol: 19 mg
- Sodium: 220 mg
- Total Carbohydrate: 34.8 g

- Protein: 3.4 g
- Fiber: 1.2 g
- Sugar: 0.6 g

Snickerdoodle Cookie Dough Bites Paleo Grain Free Egg Free Low Carb

"These low-carb snickerdoodle cookie dough bites are simple to whip up for a delicious easy healthy treat! Plus they work for almost any special diet! They're paleo, grain free, sugar free, dairy free, egg free, low carb, and THM friendly!"

Serving: 10 dough bites | Ready in: 5 m

Ingredients:

- 1/2 cup organic almond butter (use coconut butter for AIP - see above notes)
- 1 tsp organic cinnamon
- 3 Tbsp organic coconut flour
- 3 Tbsp organic coconut milk
- 3 Tbsp xylitol (see Recipe Notes for substitutes)
- 15 drops vanilla liquid stevia (see Homemade Liquid Stevia; see Recipe Notes for substitutes; if desired, sub 2 Tbsp xylitol instead)
- 1/2 tsp organic vanilla extract
- 1/4 tsp salt (optional but really adds a lot!)
- 3 Tbsp xylitol (or other preferred granulated sweetener)
- 1 1/2 tsp organic cinnamon

Direction:

1. Put all ingredients, except the topping ingredients, into a bowl.
2. Mix well until combined thoroughly.
3. Roll into balls and roll to coat in the topping.
4. Store in refrigerator.

Baklava Tartlets

"Want a quick treat that's delicious and easy to make? These tartlets will do the trick. You can serve them right away, but they're even better after chilling for about an hour in the refrigerator. Ashley Eagon, Kettering, Ohio"

Serving: 45 tartlets. | Ready in: 25 m

Ingredients:
- 3/4 cup honey
- 1/2 cup butter, melted
- 1 teaspoon ground cinnamon
- 1 teaspoon lemon juice
- 1/4 teaspoon ground cloves
- 2 cups finely chopped walnuts
- 3 packages (1.9 ounces each) frozen miniature phyllo tart shells

Direction:
1. In a small bowl, mix the first five ingredients until blended; stir in walnuts. Spoon 2 teaspoons mixture into each tart shell. Refrigerate until serving.

Nutrition Information:
- Calories: 76 calories
- Total Fat: 5g fat (1g saturated fat)

- Cholesterol: 5mg cholesterol
- Sodium: 24mg sodium
- Total Carbohydrate: 6g carbohydrate (4g sugars
- Protein: 2g protein.
- Fiber: 0 fiber) g

Seafood Gumbo

"Gumbo is one of dishes that helped make the Creole-Cajun cuisine of Louisiana so famous. We live across the border in Texas and can't get enough of this traditional Cajun version. This recipe calls for seafood, but you could also use chicken, duck or sausage. Ruth Aubey, San Antonio, Texas"

Serving: about 6 quarts. | Ready in: 50 m

Ingredients:
- 1 cup all-purpose flour
- 1 cup canola oil
- 4 cups chopped onion
- 2 cups chopped celery
- 2 cups chopped green pepper
- 1 cup sliced green onion and tops
- 4 cups chicken broth
- 8 cups water
- 4 cups sliced okra
- 2 tablespoons paprika
- 2 tablespoons salt
- 2 teaspoons oregano
- 1 teaspoon ground black pepper
- 6 cups small shrimp, rinsed and drained, or seafood of your choice

- 1 cup minced fresh parsley
- 2 tablespoons Cajun seasoning

Direction:

1. In a heavy Dutch oven, combine flour and oil until smooth. Cook over medium-high heat for 5 minutes, stirring constantly. Reduce heat to medium. Cook and stir about 10 minutes more, or until mixture is reddish-brown., Add the onion, celery, green pepper and green onions; cook and stir for 5 minutes.
2. Add the chicken broth, water, okra, paprika, salt, oregano and pepper. Bring to boil; reduce heat and simmer, covered, for 10 minutes., Add shrimp and parsley. Simmer, uncovered, about 5 minutes more or until seafood is done. Remove from heat; stir in Cajun seasoning.

Nutrition Information:

- Calories: 175 calories
- Total Fat: 9g fat (1g saturated fat)
- Cholesterol: 115mg cholesterol
- Sodium: 1574mg sodium
- Total Carbohydrate: 10g carbohydrate (3g sugars
- Protein: 12g protein.
- Fiber: 2g fiber)

New Orleans Style Spicy Shrimp

"We have family members who attended college in New Orleans. This shrimp captures their favorite flavors from the Big Easy, with the right touch of spices and heat. Susan Seymour, Valatie, New York"

Serving: 12 servings. | Ready in: 35 m

Ingredients:
- 3 medium lemons, sliced
- 2/3 cup butter, cubed
- 1/2 cup ketchup
- 1/4 cup Worcestershire sauce
- 2 tablespoons seafood seasoning
- 2 tablespoons chili garlic sauce
- 2 tablespoons Louisiana-style hot sauce
- 1 tablespoon Italian salad dressing mix
- 4 pounds uncooked shell-on shrimp (31-40 per pound)
- 2 bay leaves
- French bread

Direction:
1. Preheat oven to 350degrees. In a microwave-safe bowl, combine the first eight ingredients. Microwave, covered, on high 2-3 minutes or until butter is melted; stir until blended.,

Divide shrimp and bay leaves between two ungreased 13x9-in. baking dishes.
2. Add half of the lemon mixture to each dish; toss to combine., Bake, uncovered, 20-25 minutes or until shrimp turn pink, stirring halfway. Remove bay leaves. Serve with bread.

Nutrition Information:
- Calories: 242 calories
- Total Fat: 12g fat (7g saturated fat)
- Cholesterol: 211mg cholesterol
- Sodium: 940mg sodium
- Total Carbohydrate: 7g carbohydrate (4g sugars)
- Protein: 25g protein.
- Fiber: 0 fiber g

Ham Pineapple Kabobs

"For a twist on the usual holiday fare, we turn ham and pineapple into juicy kabobs. The marinade gets its zip from hoisin, teriyaki and soy sauces. Chandra Lane-Sirois, Kansas City, Missouri"

Serving: 12 servings. | Ready in: 45 m

Ingredients:

- 1/4 cup hoisin sauce
- 1/4 cup unsweetened pineapple juice
- 1/4 cup teriyaki sauce
- 1 tablespoon honey
- 1-1/2 teaspoons rice vinegar
- 1-1/2 teaspoons reduced-sodium soy sauce
- **KABOBS:**
- 2 pounds fully cooked boneless ham, cut into 1-inch pieces
- 1 large fresh pineapple, peeled, cored and cut into 1-in. cubes (about 4 cups)

Direction:

1. In a large resealable plastic bag, combine the first six ingredients. Add ham; seal bag and turn to coat. Refrigerate overnight., Preheat oven to 350degrees. Drain ham, reserving marinade. For glaze, pour marinade into a small saucepan; bring to a boil. Reduce heat; simmer, uncovered, 5-7 minutes or until slightly thickened, stirring occasionally.

2. Remove from heat., Meanwhile, on 12 metal or soaked wooden skewers, alternately thread ham and pineapple; place in a foil-lined 15x10x1-in.

baking pan. Brush with glaze. Bake, uncovered, 15-20 minutes or until lightly browned.

Nutrition Information:
- Calories: 144 calories
- Total Fat: 3g fat (1g saturated fat)
- Cholesterol: 39mg cholesterol
- Sodium: 1109mg sodium
- Total Carbohydrate: 15g carbohydrate (12g sugars)
- Protein: 15g protein.
- Fiber: 1g fiber

Gingerbread Spice Coffee Recipe

"A low carb coffee with gingerbread spice flavor is a perfect beverage to enjoy during the holiday festivities. It adds a nice touch of spice to coffee."

Serving: 1 | Ready in: 2 m

Ingredients:
- 1 1/2 teaspoons Sukrin Gold Fiber Syrup (or sweetener of choice)
- 1/2 teaspoon Sukrin Gold (or sweetener of choice)
- 1 tablespoon heavy cream
- 1/4 teaspoon ground ginger
- 1/8 teaspoon ground cinnamon
- 1 cup hot brewed coffee
- whipped cream
- cloves dash ground

Direction:
1. Mix together sweeteners, heavy cream, ginger, and cinnamon in large mug.
2. Add 1 cup hot brewed coffee.
3. Stir until spices have been blended into coffee.
4. Top with whipped cream and then sprinkle cloves on top

Nutrition Information:

- Calories: 108 kcal
- Total Fat: 11.2 g
- Sodium: 17 mg
- Total Carbohydrate: 1.5 g
- Protein: 1 g

Low Carb Chocolate Peppermint Cocktail

Serving: 1 | Ready in: 5 m

Ingredients:
- 1 fl oz vodka
- ½ fl oz Sugar Free Peppermint Syrup
- 1 fl oz Sugar Free Chocolate Syrup
- ½ fl oz heavy cream
- 1 tsp Swerve (granulated)
- few drops red food dye
- honey or corn syrup

Direction:
1. Mix the Swerve and red dye together on a plate. Add a little honey to a paper towel then wipe the rim of a cocktail glass. Dip the glass into the dyed sweetener.
2. In a cocktail shaker, mix together the remaining ingredients.
3. Add some ice cubes to the prepared glass and pour the shaken cocktail over the top of the ice.

Nutrition Information:
- Calories: 115 kcal
- Total Fat: 5 g
- Saturated Fat: 3 g
- Cholesterol: 20 mg

- Sodium: 25 mg
- Total Carbohydrate: 5 g

Low Carb Santa Cocktail

"A low carb festive cocktail for you to enjoy!"

Serving:2

Ingredients:
- 6 oz fresh raspberries
- 2 tbs water
- 1 tbs low carb sweetener
- 1 fl oz gin
- **ice**
- **Prosecco**
- liquid sweetener (optional)
- xylitol or granular Swerve (optional)

Direction:
1. Add raspberries, water, and sweetener to a small saucepan. Cook over a medium heat until the fruit breaks down.
2. Let cool then blitz the mixture in a blender or similar until smooth. Then push it through a sieve to remove any seeds.
3. To garnish the glasses, wipe a little liquid sweetener around the rim of each glass. Pour some xylitol onto a plate, invert the glass and dip it in.
4. To make the cocktail, add the raspberry mixture, gin, and ice to a cocktail shaker and shake well.

5. Divide the mixture between two glasses, then top up with Prosecco. Add a garnish of fresh raspberries if you like.

   Nutrition Information:
   - Calories: 90 kcal
   - Sodium: 3 mg
   - Total Carbohydrate: 10 g
   - Protein: 1 g
   - Fiber: 5 g
   - Sugar: 4 g

Part 2

Christmas Biscuits

INGREDIENTS

- 100g/3½oz unsalted butter, softened at room temperature
- 100g/3½oz caster sugar
- 1 free-range egg, lightly beaten
- 1 tsp vanilla extract
- 275g/10oz plain flour
- To decorate
- 400g/14oz icing sugar
- 3-4 tbsp water
- 2-3 drops food colourings
- Edible glitter

DIRECTIONS

1. Preheat the oven to 190C/375F/Gas 5. Line a baking tray with greaseproof paper.
2. Cream the butter and sugar together in a bowl until pale, light and fluffy.
3. Beat in the egg and vanilla extract, a little at a time, until well combined.
4. Stir in the flour until the mixture comes together as a dough.
5. Roll the dough out on a lightly floured work surface to a thickness of 1cm/½in.
6. Using biscuit cutters or a glass, cut biscuits out of the dough and carefully place onto the baking tray. To make into Christmas tree decorations, carefully make a hole in the top of the biscuit using a straw.
7. Bake the biscuits for 8-10 minutes, or until pale golden-brown. Set aside to harden for 5 minutes, then cool on a wire rack.

8. For the icing, sift the icing sugar into a large mixing bowl and stir in enough water to create a smooth mixture. Stir in the food colouring.
9. Carefully spread the icing onto the biscuits using a knife and sprinkle over the glitter. Set aside until the icing hardens.

Magical Sugar Cookies

INGREDIENTS

- 2 3/4 c.
- all-purpose flour
- 1/2 tsp.
- baking powder
- 1/4 tsp.
- kosher salt
- 1 c.
- (2 sticks) unsalted butter, at room temp
- 3/4 c.
- sugar
- 1
- large egg
- 1 1/2 tsp.
- pure vanilla extract

DIRECTIONS

1. In large bowl, whisk together flour, baking powder, and salt.
2. In another large bowl, using electric mixer, beat butter and sugar until light and fluffy, about 3 minutes. Beat in egg and then vanilla.
3. Reduce mixer speed to low and gradually add flour mixture, mixing just until incorporated. Shape dough into 2 disks and roll each between 2 sheets of waxed paper to 1/8 inches thick. Chill until firm, 30 minutes in refrigerator or 15 minutes in freezer.
4. Heat oven to 350°F. Line baking sheets with parchment paper. Using floured cookie cutters, cut out cookies. Place on prepared sheets. Reroll, chill and cut scraps.
5. Bake, rotating positions of baking sheets halfway through, until cookies are light golden brown around edges, 10 to 12 minutes. Let cool on sheets 5 min. before transferring to wire racks to cool completely.

Mocha Men And Star Cookies

INGREDIENTS

- 2 1/4 c.
- all-purpose flour
- 1/2 c.
- unsweetened cocoa powder
- 1/2 tsp.
- baking powder
- 2 tsp.
- instant espresso powder
- 1/4 tsp.
- Kosher salt
- 1 c.
- (2 sticks) unsalted butter, at room temp
- 3/4 c.
- sugar
- 1
- large egg
- 1 1/2 tsp. pure vanilla extractMelted chocolate

DIRECTIONS

1. In a large bowl, whisk together flour, cocoa powder, baking powder, espresso powder, and salt.
2. In another large bowl, using electric mixer, beat butter and sugar until light and fluffy, about 3 minutes. Beat in egg and then vanilla.
3. Reduce mixer speed to low and gradually add flour mixture, mixing just until incorporated. Shape dough into 2 disks and roll each between 2 sheets of waxed paper to 1/8 inches thick. Chill until firm, 30 minutes in refrigerator or 15 minutes in freezer.
4. Heat oven to 350°F. Line baking sheets with parchment paper. Using floured small gingerbread and star cutters, cut out cookies. Place on prepared sheets. Reroll, chill and cut scraps.
5. Bake, rotating positions of baking sheets halfway through, until edges are set, 10 to 12 minutes. Let cool on sheets 5 minutes before transferring to wire racks to cool completely. Once cool, dip half of each cookie in melted chocolate and let set.

Soft Chocolate Chip Cookies

INGREDIENTS
- 2 ¼ cups flour
- 1 teaspoon baking soda
- ¾ cup packed brown sugar
- ½ cup butter, softened
- ½ cup shortening
- ¼ cup sugar
- 1 (4 ounce) package instant vanilla pudding
- 1 teaspoon vanilla extract
- ⅛ teaspoon almond extract
- 2 eggs, beaten
- 2 cups chocolate chips

DIRECTIONS
1. Preheat oven 350 degrees.
2. Combine flour and baking soda.
3. In a large bowl beat brown sugar, sugar, butter, shortening, pudding mix, vanilla, and almond extract.
4. Mix until well blended.
5. Add eggs and mix well.
6. Beat in the flour mixture.
7. Stir in chocolate chips.
8. Drop by rounded teaspoonful and bake 10-12 minutes.

Chocolate Peppermint Pinwheel Cookies

INGREDIENTS

- ☐ BASIC DOUGH
- 3 cups all-purpose flour
- ¾ teaspoon baking powder
- ¼ teaspoon salt
- 1 cup unsalted butter, softened
- 1 cup sugar
- 1 egg, beaten
- 1 tablespoon milk
- powdered sugar, for rolling out dough
- ☐ CHOCOLATE
- 3 ounces unsweetened chocolate, melted
- 1 teaspoon vanilla extract
- ☐ PEPPERMINT
- 1 egg yolk
- 1 teaspoon peppermint extract
- ½ cup crushed candy canes or ½ cup peppermint candy
- red food coloring (optional)

DIRECTIONS
1. Sift together flour, baking powder, and salt. Set aside.
2. Place butter and sugar in large bowl of electric stand mixer and beat until light and fluffy. Add egg and milk and beat to combine. Put mixer on low speed, gradually add flour, and beat until mixture pulls away from the side of the bowl. The dough will be very stiff and crumbly at this point alost like a shortbread. Don't worry, you are adding liquid in the next steps.
3. Divide the dough in half and add chocolate and vanilla to 1 half and incorporate with hands. Add egg yolk, peppermint extract, and crushed candy to other half of dough and incorporate with hands. (If you like you can add a drop or two of red food coloring to make the dough a pppermint pink.) Cover both with plastic and chill for approximately 5-10 minutes.
4. Roll out doughs separately to approximately 1/4-inch thickness. Place peppermint dough on top of chocolate and press together around the edges. Using waxed paper or flexible cutting board underneath, roll dough into log. Wrap in wax paper and refrigerate for 2 hours or more. (I let my logs cool for 6 hours and they were very easy to slice.).
5. Preheat oven to 375 degrees.
6. Remove dough from the refrigerator and cut into 1/4-inch slices. Place cookies 1-inch apart on greased baking sheet, parchment, or silicone baking mat and bake for 12 to 13 minutes, rotating the pan halfway through cooking time. Remove from oven and let sit on baking sheet for 2 minutes, then move to a wire rack to cool completely.

The Most Wonderful Gingerbread Cookies

INGREDIENTS

- 3 cups all-purpose flour
- 1 ½ teaspoons baking powder
- ¾ teaspoon baking soda
- ¼ teaspoon salt
- 1 tablespoon ground ginger
- 1 ¾ teaspoons ground cinnamon
- ¼ teaspoon ground cloves
- 6 tablespoons unsalted butter
- ¾ cup dark brown sugar
- 1 large egg
- ½ cup molasses
- 2 teaspoons vanilla
- 1 teaspoon finely grated lemon zest (optional)

DIRECTIONS
1. In a small bowl, whisk together flour, baking powder, baking soda, salt, ginger, cinnamon, and cloves until well blended.
2. In a large bowl (KitchenAid's great for this) beat butter, brown sugar, and egg on medium speed until well blended.
3. Add molasses, vanilla, and lemon zest and continue to mix until well blended.
4. Gradually stir in dry ingredients until blended and smooth.
5. Divide dough in half and wrap each half in plastic and let stand at room temperature for at least 2 hours or up to 8 hours.
6. Preheat oven to 375 deg. Prepare baking sheets by lining with parchment paper.
7. (Dough can be stored in the refrigerator for up to 4 days, but in this case it should be refrigerated. Return to room temp before using.) Preheat oven to 375°.
8. Grease or line cookie sheets with parchment paper.
9. Place 1 portion of the dough on a lightly floured surface.
10. Sprinkle flour over dough and rolling pin.
11. Roll dough to a scant 1/4-inch thick.
12. Use additional flour to avoid sticking.
13. Cut out cookies with desired cutter-- the ginger bread man is our favorite of course.
14. Space cookies 1 1/2-inches apart.
15. Bake 1 sheet at a time for 7-10 minutes (the lower time will give you softer cookies-- very good!).
16. Remove cookie sheet from oven and allow the cookies to stand until the cookies are firm enough to move to a wire rack.
17. After cookies are cool you may decorate them any way you like.

18. I usually brush them with a powdered sugar glaze when I am in a hurry, but they look wonderful decorated with Royal icing.

Chewy Chocolate Chip Oatmeal Cookies

INGREDIENTS
- 1 cup butter, softened
- 1 cup packed light brown sugar
- $\frac{1}{3}$ cup white sugar
- 2 eggs
- 2 teaspoons vanilla extract
- 1 $\frac{1}{2}$ cups all-purpose flour
- 1 teaspoon baking soda
- $\frac{1}{2}$ teaspoon salt
- 3 cups quick-cooking oats
- 1 cup chopped walnuts
- 1 cup semi-sweet chocolate chips
- 1 $\frac{1}{2}$ teaspoons ground cinnamon (optional)

DIRECTIONS
1. Preheat the oven to 325°F.
2. In a large bowl,sift together flour, baking soda and salt. Set aside.
3. In another another bowl, cream together butter, brown sugar and white sugar until smooth. Beat in eggs one at a time, then stir in vanilla. Stir dry ingredients in the cream mixture until just blended. mix in quick oats, walnuts and chocolate chips.
4. Drop by heaping spoonfuls onto ungreased baking sheet.
5. Bake for 13 minutes in the preheated oven. Allow cookies to cool on baking sheet for 5 minutes before transferring to a wire rack to cool completely.

Uncle Bill's Whipped Shortbread Cookies

INGREDIENTS

- 1 cup butter, softened
- 1 ½ cups all-purpose flour
- ½ cup icing sugar or ½ cup powdered sugar
- 1 teaspoon vanilla extract (optional)
- ¼ cup red maraschino cherry

¼ cup green maraschino cherry

DIRECTIONS
1. Preheat oven to 350 degrees F.
2. In a mixing bowl and using an electric mixer, combine butter, flour, icing sugar and vanilla extract; mix until mixture is a smooth consistency.
3. Prepare cookie sheets with parchment paper.
4. Spoon out dough onto parchment lined cookie sheets by teaspoonfuls or by tablespoons for larger cookies, spacing about 2 inches apart.
5. Cut maraschino cherries into quarters and place one piece in the middle of each cookie, alternating with red and green cherries.
6. Bake in preheated 350 F oven for 13 to 15 minutes or until bottom of cookies are lightly browned, DO NOT OVERBAKE.
7. Remove from oven and let cool on cookie sheet for about 5 minutes.
8. Transfer onto wire racks to finish cooling.
9. Store in a container with a lid and separate each layer with wax paper

Pecan Puffs

INGREDIENTS
- $1/2$ cup salted butter, softened
- 2 tablespoons sugar
- 1 teaspoon vanilla
- $3/4$ cup finely chopped pecans
- 1 cup cake flour
- $1/4$ teaspoon salt (or less)
- powdered sugar, reserved

DIRECTIONS
1. Preheat oven to 300°.
2. Put on some Christmas music.
3. Chop pecan in a food processor or by knife.
4. Beat butter until soft with a mixer. Add sugar, vanilla, and pecans. Carefully add flour and blend well.
5. Coat hands with flour. Use a teaspoon scoop or a teaspoon and shape into cherry-size and place on a parchment-lined or greased cookie sheet.
6. Bake at 300° 15-20 minutes.
7. (These should be light in color. Do not brown!) While cookies are still quite warm, roll them in confectioner's sugar. When cool, roll in confectioner's sugar again.

Christmas Chocolate Cherry Cookies

INGREDIENTS
- 1 cup shortening
- 1 ½ cups white sugar
- 2 large eggs
- 1 teaspoon almond extract
- 2 cups flour
- 1 teaspoon baking powder
- ¼ teaspoon salt
- 1 cup semi-sweet chocolate chips
- 1 ½ cups coconut

1 ½ cups chopped maraschino cherries

DIRECTIONS
1. Cream shortening and sugar in large bowl with electric mixer until well blended.
2. Add eggs and almond extract, beating on medium speed until light and fluffy; about 2 minutes.
3. Combine flour, baking powder and salt. Add to creamed mixture gradually, beating on low speed just until blended. Fold in chips, coconut and cherries.

   Drop dough by spoonfuls onto greased cookie sheets. Bake at 350° for 12-15 minutes or until lightly browned around edges.

White Chocolate Chip Cranberry Oatmeal Cookies

INGREDIENTS
- ¾ cup sugar
- ¼ cup packed brown sugar
- ½ cup butter, softened
- 1 large egg
- ½ teaspoon vanilla extract
- ½ teaspoon cinnamon
- ½ teaspoon baking soda
- ¼ teaspoon salt
- 1 cup all-purpose flour
- 1 ½ cups quick-cooking oats (not instant)
- ¾ cup dried cranberries
- 6 ounces white chocolate chips

DIRECTIONS
1. Preheat oven to 375°F.
2. In a large bowl using an electric mixer combine the sugar, brown sugar and butter; mix well to cream together.
3. Add in egg and vanilla extract and mix until combined.
4. Add the cinnamon, baking soda, salt and flour and mix well.
5. Fold in the oatmeal, dried cranberries and white chocolate chips- making sure that all ingredients are uniformly distributed.
6. Roll dough into 1-inch balls and place 3 inches apart onto a greased cookie sheet and bake at 375° for 10-12 minutes, just until the edges are lightly golden.
7. Remove from oven and let cool for 2-3 minutes on the cookie sheet, then transfer cookies to cooling rack.

Peanut Butter Blossoms

INGREDIENTS
- 1 ¾ cups flour
- 1 teaspoon baking soda
- ½ teaspoon salt
- ½ cup sugar
- ½ cup brown sugar
- 1 teaspoon vanilla
- ½ cup shortening
- ½ cup peanut butter
- 1 egg
- 2 tablespoons milk
- additional sugar

DIRECTIONS
1. Combine shortening, sugars, egg, vanilla and peanut butter.
2. Add dry ingredients and milk.
3. Shape dough into small balls, then roll in sugar.
4. Place on an ungreased cookie sheet.
5. Bake 10 minutes at 350.
6. Place a kiss in middle of each cookie pressing until the edges crack.

Penguin Cookies

INGREDIENTS
- 24 Town House Crackers
- creamy peanut butter (about 1 tsp. per cookie)
- 1 (16 oz) pkg, chocolate candy coating
- 12 bright white chocolate candy melt wafers
- orange candy coated peanut butter candies (2 candies for feet and 1/2 candy for beak)
- candy eyes (2 per cookie)

DIRECTIONS

1. Lay out a couple large sheets of waxed paper on your work surface. Prepare your decorations - its helpful to place each decoration in small bowls so they are ready to go when you need them. The chocolate will cool and harden within minutes, so you'll need everything at your fingertips to work quickly.

2. Begin making the cracker sandwiches by spreading one cracker with 1 tsp. of peanut butter. Place the second cracker on top to create a sandwich. Repeat this process for all of your cookies.

3. Next, melt the chocolate candy coating according to package directions. Dip each of the cracker sandwiches into the chocolate coating, covering the entire outer surface. Place on the waxed paper. While the chocolate is still wet, place a white chocolate wafer on the bottom half of the cookie for the penguin tummy. Place two orange candies at the bottom for the feet, two eyes at the top, and a 1/2 orange candy for the beak.

4. Let the chocolate cool and set completely before handling. Keep cookies at room temperature or freeze.

Caramel Macchiato Cookies

INGREDIENTS
- 1 1/2 cup Butter , unsalted, room temperature
- 1 cup Sugar
- 1 Egg , large
- 3 1/4 cups All-purpose flour
- 4 teaspoon Starbucks VIA Instant Latte White Chocolate Mocha
- 16 Caramels
- 2 tablespoon Heavy Cream
- 1/2 cup Chocolate Chips

DIRECTIONS
1. Preheat oven to 350F.
2. In a large bowl use a mixer to beat the butter and sugar together.
3. Add egg and continue to mix until all ingredients are thoroughly combined.
4. In a small bowl mix together flour and coffee powder.
5. Turn mixer to low and add flour mixture. Do not over mix. Stop as soon as flour is combined.
6. Make dough into 1-inch balls and place on a baking sheet 3-4 inches apart.
7. Use the back of a teaspoon, or your thumb, to press down in the center of the ball to make an indentation.
8. Bake until cookies are golden brown around edges, 18 - 20 minutes.
9. When cookies come out of the oven use the back of the teaspoon to gently press the centers down again.
10. Let the cookies cool completely on a wire rack.
11. Unwrap caramel candies and place them in a microwave safe bowl. Add heavy cream and microwave, 15 seconds at a time, until melted.

12. Once the cookies have cooled fill each indentation with the caramel.
13. Let caramel cool and then place the chocolate chips in a microwaveable dish and microwave for 15 seconds at a time until they are completely melted. Drizzle the top of the cookies with melted chocolate.
14. Once chocolate has hardened serve and enjoy!

Chocolate Crinkle Peppermint Blossom

INGREDIENTS

- 1/2 c vegetable oil
- 4 oz. unsweetened chocolate, melted and cooled
- 2 c sugar
- 2 t vanilla
- 4 eggs
- 2 c all-purpose flour
- 2 t baking powder
- 1/2 t salt
- 1/2 c powdered sugar
- 10 oz bag of Hershey's candy cane Kisses

DIRECTIONS

1. in a large mixing bowl combine oil, chocolate, sugar and vanilla
2. add eggs one at a time
3. in a med bowl combine flour, baking powder, and salt
4. add flour mixture into the chocolate mixture until combined
5. cover and refrigerate for 3 hours or overnight
6. preheat oven to 350 degrees
7. pour powdered sugar into a shallow bowl
8. roll balls of dough 1 tablespoon big and roll in the powdered sugar
9. place on a cookie sheet 2 inches apart and bake for 10 min
10. while cookies are baking remove kisses from their wrappers and have nearby
11. as soon as cookies come out of the oven place a kiss in the center of each cookie

12. allow to cool for 5 min on cookie sheet and then remove to a cooling rack to finish

Triple Chocolate Peppermint Cookies

INGREDIENTS

- 1 1/4 Cups unsalted butter, softened
- 2 Cups granulated sugar
- 2 Large eggs
- 1 Tablespoon pure vanilla extract
- 2 Cups unbleached, all-purpose flour
- 3/4 cups cocoa powder
- 1 1/2 Teaspoons baking soda
- 1 teaspoon salt
- 9.90 Ounce bag White Chocolate Peppermint M&Ms (about 1 1/2 cups)
- 10 Ounce bag Ghirardelli bittersweet chocolate chips

DIRECTIONS

1. Preheat oven to 350 degrees. Place parchment paper/silpat on baking sheets, set aside.
2. Beat butter, eggs, sugar, and vanilla extract together in a large bowl until light and fluffy.
3. Combine the cocoa powder, flour, baking soda, and salt then add to the butter mixture. Beat just until well combined.
4. Stir in M&Ms and chocolate chips.
5. Using a #30 cookie scoop {one ounce} drop rounded cookies onto prepared baking sheets {9 per pan}.
6. Bake in preheated oven until set, but still soft and chewy, about 16 minutes.
7. Remove from oven and allow to cool on baking sheet for 3 minutes before moving to a wire cooling rack to cool completely.
8. Store in a sealed container.

Christmas Sugar Cookie Recipe

INGREDIENTS

- 2¼ cups white sugar
- 3 sticks butter - room temperature
- 3 eggs
- 1 TBL vanilla
- 1¼ tsp. baking powder
- ¾ tsp. salt
- 5 cups flour

DIRECTIONS

1. In a mixing bowl with a paddle attachment, cream together butter and sugar until fluffy.
2. Add eggs and vanilla and mix together until all incorporated.
3. Sift together dry ingredients and slowly add to sugar mixture and mix until all combined.
4. Dump dough out onto plastic wrap.
5. Wrap up and chill in fridge for 30 minutes.
6. (Can be refrigerated for up to 1 week. Just remove from fridge and set out for 15 minutes before rolling out.)
7. Unwrap dough onto a floured surface and roll out to ¼ to ½ inch thick.
8. Cut out shapes with cookie cutters and place on baking sheet 2 inches apart.
9. Bake at 350 degrees for 8 - 10 minutes.
10. (I remove mine before edges start to brown.)
11. Cool on cookie sheet for 5 minutes and then place on parchment or cooling rack to finish cooling.
12. Once completely cooled, time to decorate!

Peppermint Twist Macarons

INGREDIENTS
COOKIES:

- 1 cup caster sugar*
- 3/4 cup almond flour
- 2 egg whites , room temperature
- pinch cream of tartar
- 1/4 cup caster sugar

FILLING

- 1/4 cup **butter** , softened
- 1 cup powdered sugar
- 1 teaspoon vanilla or peppermint extract
- 1 tablespoon milk
- 1/2 cup candy canes , crushed

DIRECTIONS

1. In food processor or blender, pulse powdered sugar and almond flour for one minute, scraping down sides, until well blended and mixture starts to cling together.
2. Transfer to a sifter, sift into a small bowl. Repeat again, set aside.
3. In the bowl of a stand mixer or a large metal mixing bowl, whip egg whites until white and frothy. Add pinch of cream of tartar and continue to whip until mixture has increased in size. See **How to Choose the Right Mixing Bowl** for reasons why metal is so important for egg whites. Continue to whip and add caster sugar, continue whipping for 5 minutes or until mixture is stiff and peaks form and stand on their own without falling.

4. At this point, sift almond flour mixture for a third time directly into the meringue base.
5. Preheat oven to 375 degrees. Prepare a large pastry/frosting bag with a ¾ inch round tip and fill with meringue. Pipe 1 ½ rounds to a parchment paper lined baking sheet. Attempt to whip the tip around and prevent little nubs on the tops. I don't always do such a good job of this- but then again, they still look pretty!
6. Tap baking sheet several times on the counter to get air bubbles out. Allow to sit at room temperature for 5 minutes.
7. At the same time that you place your cookies into the oven, reduce heat to 325 degrees. Bake for 10-12 minutes or until meringues are crispy on the outside and baked into the classic meringue shape with a little ridge along the bottom.
8. Remove and allow to cool for 10 minutes before removing from baking sheet. Macarons should easily twist off parchment paper, but if not, spray water between parchment paper and baking sheet, the steam will release the cookies.
9. Allow to cool fully before attempting to sandwich.
10. Make frosting by combining softened butter, powdered sugar and vanilla extract. Add milk, 1 teaspoon at a time, until frosting is a spreadable consistency. Leave at room temperature until ready to assemble.
11. Pair cookies with a similar size with a heaping teaspoon of frosting between each. Make sure you have enough in the center that frosting oozes out the side; this will be what candy canes crumbles will stick to.
12. Spread crushed candy canes on a plate or in a shallow bowl. Roll sides of macarons in crumbles, allowing them to stick to center frosting.

13. Store peppermint twist macarons in refrigerator.

Turtle Snickerdoodles

INGREDIENTS
- 2 3/4 cup all-purpose flour
- 1/2 teaspoon Salt
- 2 teaspoon baking powder
- 1 cup butter unsalted, room temp.
- 1 1/2 cup Sugar
- 2 eggs large
- 1 teaspoon vanilla
- ½ teaspoon cinnamon
- 1 7oz bag of Pecan halves
- 1 bag Rolo or other chocolate and caramel candies

DIRECTIONS

1. Preheat oven to 400F.
2. In a mixing bowl cream butter and sugar together until smooth.
3. Add eggs one at a time, mixing until just combined.
4. Add vanilla and continue mixing.
5. In a separate bowl combine flour, baking powder, cinnamon, and salt.
6. Add flour mixture to butter mixture and beat until the dough is smooth.
7. Refrigerate for 30 minutes - 1 hour.
8. Line a baking sheet with parchment paper or a silpat mat.
9. Roll dough into 1 inch balls and gently press down on them with the bottom of a glass, or the palm of your hand to flatten them slightly.

10. Bake for 6 minutes, then remove cookies from oven and press an unwrapped rolo into the center of each cookie.
11. Place cookies back in the oven for 2 minutes.
12. Remove from oven and press a pecan half into each roll, flattening it.
13. Move cookies to a wire rack and let cool completely.

Black-And-White Cookies

INGREDIENTS

5 cups cake flour

1 tsp. baking powder

$\frac{1}{2}$ tsp. kosher salt

1 $\frac{3}{4}$ cups sugar

16 tbsp. unsalted butter, softened

4 eggs

1 cup milk

1 tsp. vanilla extract

1 (1-lb.) box confectioners' sugar, sifted

3 oz. unsweetened chocolate, finely chopped

DIRECTIONS

Heat the oven to 375°. In a large bowl, whisk together flour, baking powder, and salt; set aside. In another bowl, combine sugar and butter, and beat with an electric mixer on medium-high speed until pale and fluffy, about 3 minutes. Add eggs one at a time, beating after each addition, and beat until smooth. Add milk, vanilla, and the reserved flour mixture; beat on low speed until just combined.

Use an ice cream scoop or a $\frac{1}{4}$-cup measuring cup to divide the dough into roughly 24 portions. Transfer dough portions to parchment paper-lined baking sheets, spacing the portions 2" apart. Bake until cookies are set and lightly browned at the edges, about 15 minutes. Let cool completely.

Meanwhile, make the icing: Whisk together the confectioners' sugar and $\frac{1}{3}$ cup boiling water in a medium glass bowl to make a smooth glaze (this will be the white icing). Working with one cookie at a time, hold the cookie horizontally, gently gripping it by the edges, and dip the top in the white glaze (you'll get some icing on your fingers); then return the cookie to the baking sheet to let the icing set. Meanwhile, make the black icing by adding the chocolate to the remaining white glaze. Microwave the mixture for about 45 seconds; stir to combine. Dip each white-glazed cookie vertically halfway into the chocolate glaze and transfer to the baking sheet. Let the chocolate glaze set completely before serving.

Anise-Almond Sprinkle Cookies

INGREDIENTS

8 tbsp. unsalted butter, softened

$\frac{1}{2}$ cup sugar

3 eggs

3 tbsp. milk

1 tbsp. vanilla extract

2 tsp. almond extract

2 $\frac{1}{2}$ cups flour

1 tbsp. baking powder

$\frac{1}{8}$ tsp. kosher salt

For the Glaze

2 cups confectioners' sugar

3 tbsp. Pernod

Rainbow nonpareils

DIRECTIONS

Make the cookies: Heat oven to 350°. Cream the butter and sugar with hand mixer; add eggs one at a time. Add milk and extracts, then flour, baking powder, and salt. Roll into 1-tbsp. balls; bake 10 minutes or until browned on the bottom. Allow to cool before glazing.

Make the glaze: Whisk confectioners' sugar and Pernod together to form a smooth glaze; add water to thin as needed. Dip cookies in glaze and top with nonpareils.

Gingerbread Cookies

INGREDIENTS

2 cups flour, plus more for dusting

2 cups whole wheat flour

1 $\frac{1}{2}$ tbsp. ground ginger

1 tsp. ground cinnamon

1 tsp. baking soda

$\frac{1}{4}$ tsp. ground cloves

$\frac{1}{4}$ tsp. kosher salt

8 tbsp. unsalted butter, softened

$\frac{1}{2}$ cup brown sugar

$\frac{1}{2}$ cup molasses

1 egg white

3 cups confectioners' sugar

DIRECTIONS

Combine flours, ginger, cinnamon, baking soda, cloves, and salt; set aside. Using an electric hand mixer, beat butter and sugar until fluffy. Add molasses and $\frac{1}{2}$ cup water. Slowly add flour mixture and mix until combined. Cover with plastic wrap and refrigerate 1 hour.

Preheat oven to 350°. On a lightly floured surface, roll dough out into a 12" circle, $\frac{1}{4}$" thick. Cut cookies into shapes. Place onto an ungreased baking tray and bake 12 minutes, or until the cookies do not leave an indentation when lightly touched. Cool on rack. Whisk egg white until thick and foamy. Add in confectioners' sugar and $\frac{1}{4}$-$\frac{1}{2}$ tsp. water and whisk until smooth. Place in a piping bag with $\frac{1}{8}$" circle tip and decorate as desired.

Cherry Snowball Cookies

INGREDIENTS

2 cups flour

1 tsp. baking powder

$\frac{1}{4}$ tsp. kosher salt

16 tbsp. unsalted butter, softened

$\frac{1}{4}$ cup confectioners' sugar

$\frac{1}{2}$ cup almond paste

1 tsp. vanilla extract

1 egg

1 cup (about 30) pitted Luxardo cherries, drained

2 cups coarse decorating sugar

DIRECTIONS

Heat oven to 350°. Whisk flour, baking powder, and salt in a bowl. Using a hand mixer, beat butter and confectioners' sugar in another bowl until fluffy. Mix in almond paste, vanilla, and egg. Slowly add dry ingredients until dough forms. Roll dough into thirty 1-oz. balls. Working with 1 ball at a time, press thumb into dough and place a cherry in the center; roll dough into a ball, encasing cherry. Roll cookies in decorating sugar and place on parchment paper-lined baking sheets; bake until golden, about 20 minutes. Let cookies cool completely.

Norwegian Wafer Cookies

INGREDIENTS

- 1 cup sugar
- 4 eggs
- 9 tbsp. unsalted butter, melted and cooled
- 1 tsp. ground cardamom
- $\frac{1}{2}$ tsp. vanilla extract
- $1\frac{1}{2}$ cups flour
- 2 tbsp. baking powder
- Sweeted whipped cream
- Confectioners' sugar, to garnish

DIRECTIONS

In a bowl, whisk together sugar and eggs. Whisk in 8 tbsp. butter, cardamom, and vanilla. Sift flour and baking powder into batter; whisk. Heat a krumkake maker; brush with remaining butter. Add 1 heaping tbsp. batter to each mold. Close cover; cook until wafers are golden, 45–60 seconds. Wrap 1 wafer around a krumkake cone; let harden. Remove from cone; repeat. Repeat with remaining batter. Let cool. Pipe cream into krumkakes; dust with sugar.

Meringue Cookies

INGREDIENTS
- 3egg whites
- 1cup sugar
- ¼teaspoon salt
- 1teaspoon vanilla

DIRECTIONS
1. Heat oven to 300 degrees.
2. Blend egg whites, sugar, salt and vanilla in top of double boiler.
3. Place over boiling water; beat with rotary beater, scraping bottom and side of pan occasionally, until mixture forms stiff peaks.
4. Drop mixture by teaspoonfuls onto 2 lightly greased baking sheets.
5. (Drop all mixture onto the 2 baking sheets; bake only 1 baking sheet at a time.) Bake 12 to 15 minutes or until light brown.
6. Immediately remove from baking sheet.

Chocolate Almond Crisps

INGREDIENTS
- 2 cups ground blanched almonds
- 1 1/2 cups icing sugar
- 4 tablespoons cocoa powder
- 2 1/2 teaspoons ground cinnamon
- 1/8 teaspoon ground cloves
- 3 ounces unsweetened chocolate
- 1/2 teaspoon almond extract
- 2 large egg whites

DIRECTIONS
1. Preheat the oven to 325°F.
2. Line a couple of cookie trays with parchment paper.
3. In a food processor, process the almonds with the sugar until finely ground.
4. Add the cocoa, spices and broken up chocolate and process again, until the chocolate is finely ground.
5. Process in the egg whites and the extract until it blends and forms a mass.
6. Remove the dough, let sit for about 5 minutes.
7. Roll out on a board sprinkled with icing sugar.
8. Cut with cookie cutters and place on the trays.
9. Bake in the centre of the oven for 10 to 12 minutes until almost firm and slightly puffed; they should not be browned.
10. Let cool then peel from the paper.

Italian Christmas Cookies

- ☐ INGREDIENTS
- 1cup butter, softened
- 2cups sugar
- 3eggs
- 1(15 ounce) carton ricotta cheese
- 2teaspoons vanilla extract
- 4cups all-purpose flour
- 1teaspoon salt
- 1teaspoon baking soda
- ☐ FROSTING
- ¼cup butter, softened
- 3 -4cups confectioners' sugar
- ½teaspoon vanilla extract
- 3 -4tablespoons milk
- colored sprinkles

DIRECTIONS

1. In a bowl, cream butter and sugar. Add the eggs, one at a time, beating well after each addition.
2. Beat in ricotta and vanilla.
3. Combine flour, salt and baking soda; gradually add to creamed mixture.
4. Drop by rounded teaspoonfuls 2 inches apart onto greased baking sheets. Bake at 350° for 10-12 minutes or until lightly browned.
5. Remove to wire racks to cool.
6. In a bowl, cream butter, sugar and vanilla. Add enough milk until frosting reaches spreading consistency. Frost cooled cookies and immediately decorate with sprinkles. Store in the refrigerator.

The Bestest Butter Cookies

INGREDIENTS
- 2/3 cup butter, softened
- 1/2 cup sugar
- 1 egg, beaten well
- 1/2 teaspoon vanilla
- 1 3/4 cups all-purpose flour
- 1/2 teaspoon baking powder
  decorator icing, in various colors or confectioner's sugar icing, colored with food coloring (optional)

DIRECTIONS
1. Cream butter and sugar well.
2. Add egg and vanilla and beat well.
3. Combine baking powder and flour.
4. Add gradually to creamed mixture.
5. Chill until firm.
6. Preheat oven to 400 degrees.
7. Roll out dough to about 1/4" thickness and cut into desired shapes.
8. Bake for 6 to 8 minutes.
9. When cool, decorate with frosting or icing if desired.

Christmas Mint Cookies

INGREDIENTS
- $\frac{1}{2}$lb Melting Chocolate baking chocolate
- 2 -3drops peppermint extract

1package Ritz cracker

DIRECTIONS
1. Melt Chocolate over low heat.
2. Add 2 to 3 drops of Peppermint oil.
3. You do not need alot so make sure they are small drops.
4. Mix.
5. Line a cookies sheet with foil.
6. Dip Crackers into Chocolate,Cover and lay on cookie sheet make sure they do not touch.
7. Chill until firm.

Raspberry Swirl Cookies

INGREDIENTS

- $1/2$ cup butter, softened (not margarine)
- 1 cup sugar
- 1 large egg
- 1 teaspoon vanilla extract
- 2 cups flour
- 1 teaspoon baking powder
- $1/4$ teaspoon salt

RASPBERRY FILLING

- $3/4$ cup raspberry jam
- $1/2$ cup coconut
  $1/3$ cup finely chopped walnuts

DIRECTIONS

1. Stir butter until smooth. Beat in sugar. Add egg and vanilla; beat well.
2. In a separate bowl combine flour, baking powder, and salt. Add to creamed mixture, beating well.
3. Shape dough into a ball. Wrap in plastic wrap and chill 2 hours.
4. Meanwhile, combine all ingredients for raspberry filling.
5. On floured wax paper roll dough into a 12x9 inch rectangle. Spread Raspberry Filling evenly to within 1/2-inch of edges. Carefully roll dough jellyroll fashion, starting at long end and peeling wax paper from dough as you roll. Pinch side seam to seal (leave ends open). Wrap in plastic wrap and chill 1 hour.
6. Unwrap and cut into 1/4-inch slices. Place 2-inches apart on greased cookies sheets. Bake at 375° for 8-10 minutes or just before cookies begin to brown.

Elaine's Holiday Cut Out Sugar Cookies

INGREDIENTS
- 1 cup butter
- 1 ½ cups sugar
- 2 eggs
- 2 teaspoons vanilla
- 3 ½ cups flour
- 1 teaspoon baking powder
- ½ teaspoon salt

DIRECTIONS
1. Preheat oven to 375.
2. Cream butter and sugar.
3. Add eggs and vanilla. Mix well.
4. Add flour, baking powder and salt. Mix well.
5. Refrigerate for at least 1 hour, to chill dough before rolling.
6. Roll dough thickly. (about 1/4"). If you roll them too thin, they are hard to work with.
7. Cut shapes, and put on an ungreased baking sheet.
8. Bake 10-12 minutes.
9. Cool on rack.
10. Frost with your favorite frosting, icing, or glaze.

Peppermint Christmas Cookies

INGREDIENTS
- ¾ cup soft butter
- ¾ cup icing sugar
- 1 egg
- 1 teaspoon vanilla
- 2 teaspoons peppermint extract
- ¼ teaspoon salt
- 1 teaspoon green food coloring or 1 teaspoon red food coloring (paste colouring gives a deep shade)
- 1 ¾ cups flour
- 30 chocolate Hershey chocolate kisses or 30 chocolate rosettes or 30 chocolate wafers

DIRECTIONS
1. Cream together butter, sugar, egg, vanilla, and salt.
2. Add coloring and mix well to distribute color evenly.
3. Stir in flour.
4. Shape in 1 inch balls.
5. Place 2 inches apart on ungreased cookie sheet.
6. Flatten each by pressing a chocolate in each center.
7. Bake at 350 degrees for 10 minutes, or until bottom starts to brown.

Christmas Gingerbread Cookies

INGREDIENTS

- 3 cups flour
- 2 teaspoons ground ginger
- 1 teaspoon ground cinnamon
- 1/2 teaspoon ground cloves
- 1/2 teaspoon ground nutmeg
- 1/2 teaspoon baking soda
- 1/4 teaspoon salt
- 1/2 cup butter, softened
- 1/2 cup packed light brown sugar
- 3/4 cup unsulfured molasses
- 1 large egg

DIRECTIONS

1. Sift flour, ginger, cinnamon, cloves, nutmeg, baking soda and salt together. Set aside.
2. Beat butter and sugar together until light and fluffy.
3. Beat in molasses and egg.
4. Gradually add flour mixture to make a soft dough.
5. Wrap dough in plastic wrap and refrigerate at least 4 hours, or overnight.
6. Preheat oven to 350°F.
7. On a lightly floured board, roll dough out to about 1/4" thickness. Do not roll too thin.
8. Cut out shapes with cookie cutters.
9. Place on lightly greased baking sheets.
10. Bake for about 8 minutes, or until just firm when pressed. Do not overbake.
11. Cool 2 minutes on baking sheet.

12. Remove and place on racks to finish cooling.

Cake Mix Christmas Cookies

INGREDIENTS

- 1 (18 ounce) package cake mix (chocolate, cherry, spice, banana, lemon of your choice)
- 2 large eggs
- ½ cup shortening
- 1 tablespoon water
- ½ cup chopped nuts or ½ cup coconut or ½ cup dried cranberries or ½ cup raisins

DIRECTIONS

1. Mix all together.
2. Shape in 1" balls and roll in powdered sugar (optional).
3. You may want to chill dough before rolling. Place on parchment lined baking sheet.
4. Bake 10-12 minutes at 375°F.

Jam-Filled Christmas Cookies

INGREDIENTS
- ¾ cup walnut pieces
- 1 ½ cups all-purpose flour, divided
- ½ cup cold butter or ½ cup margarine, cut in chunks
- ½ cup icing sugar
- ½ teaspoon almond extract
- 1 large egg
- ½ cup seedless raspberry jam (or jam of your choice)

DIRECTIONS
1. Preheat oven to 350F; line cookie sheets with parchment paper and set aside.
2. In a food processor fitted with steel blade, process walnuts and 1/4 cup of the flour until nuts are quite finely chopped; remove from processor into a dish and set aside.
3. Place remaining flour into food processor, along with butter and icing sugar; process until mixture has a crumbly texture, about 10 seconds or so.
4. Return nut mixture to food processor, along with almond extract and the egg.
5. Process until entire mixture is combined; 15 seconds or so.
6. Make one-inch balls from mixture and place on prepared cookie sheet; using the end of a wooden spoon, make an indentation into each cookie.
7. Fill each hole with a wee bit of jam; I prefer seedless raspberry, but will use strawberry too-- I find the red jams suit the holiday season, but you can use any jam you want.
8. Bake in preheated oven for 15 to 18 minutes, or until golden brown.

Melomakarona (A Greek Christmas Cookie)

INGREDIENTS

- 1 ½ cups light olive oil or 1 ½ cups corn oil
- ½ cup butter, at room temperature
- 1 cup beer (or more) or 1 cup orange juice (or more)
- 1 tablespoon ground cinnamon
- 1 ½ teaspoons ground cloves
- 2 oranges, zest of, grated
- 1 cup sugar
- 2 cups fine ground semolina (cream of wheat or farina)
- 6 cups flour
- ½ teaspoon baking soda
- ½ teaspoon baking powder
- 1 teaspoon salt

☐ SYRUP

- 1 ½ cups sugar
- 1 ½ cups greek thyme honey
- 1 cup water
- ¾ cup walnuts, finely chopped

DIRECTIONS

1. Put the corn oil, butter, beer (or orange juice), cinnamon, cloves, orange peel and sugar in a mixing bowl and beat until they are thoroughly blended.
2. Sift about one cup of flour with the baking soda, baking powder and salt and blend into the oil mixture.
3. Add the semolina, a cup at a time, into this mixture.
4. Add enough of the remaining flour, a cup at a time, until you get a rather firm dough (you may need a bit more or less than the amount of flour mentioned in the ingredients list).

5. Use your hands to do the mixing, as an electric mixer will be useless after the first two or three cups of flour have been added.
6. Roll the dough into cylinders, about two inches long and one inch in diameter, flatten them with your hands, and place them on cookie sheets that have been greased with a little olive oil.
7. Bake at 350 degree Fahrenheit for half an hour.
8. Remove the cookies from the oven and pour hot syrup over them.
9. Lay the cookies out in a rimmed baking pan large enough to contain them and pour the hot syrup over the cookies, sprinkle them with the chopped walnuts and let them soak overnight.
10. (Alternatively, if you do not have enough rimmed baking sheets to accommodate all the cookies, you can dip them in batches directly into the hot syrup - keeping the syrup at the lowest possible simmer - and allow to soak in the syrup for 8-10 minutes; remove with a slotted spoon).
11. For the syrup: mix the sugar, honey and water, and bring to a boil.
12. Cook on low heat for four minutes and skim off the foam that forms on top.
13. The next day put them on your prettiest platter, sprinkle each layer evenly with the finely chopped walnuts and wrap with plastic wrap (or put in an airtight container) and serve.

Christmas Gingerbread Cookies

INGREDIENTS

- ☐ FIRST BOWL
- $2/3$ cup shortening
- $1/2$ cup brown sugar, firmly packed
- 1 teaspoon cinnamon
- $1/4$ teaspoon ground cloves
- 2 $1/2$ teaspoons ground ginger
- 1 pinch salt
- $3/4$ cup molasses
- ☐ SECOND BOWL
- 1 large egg
- 3 cups flour
- $1/2$ teaspoon baking powder
- 1 teaspoon baking soda

DIRECTIONS

1. Mix first bowl ingredients together until it becomes a creamy brown batter.
2. Sift second bowl ingredients; add to the wet batter a little at a time.
3. Mix together until it becomes a crumby dough.
4. Make the dough into a ball and chill for an hour.
5. When ready, cover the dough in flour and place on a heavy floured surface.
6. Knead dough with the palms of your hand and roll it out.
7. Cut into desired shapes.
8. Cook for 10-15 minute until golden brown.

Swedish Christmas Cookies

INGREDIENTS
- 2 ½ cups all-purpose flour
- 2 teaspoons ground cardamom
- ¼ teaspoon fine salt
- 1 cup unsalted butter (2 sticks)
- 1 cup confectioners' sugar
- 1 large egg, room temperature
- 1 tablespoon pure vanilla extract
- 1 teaspoon finely grated lemon zest
- colored crystal sugar or chopped toasted pecans

DIRECTIONS
1. Whisk the flour, cardamom, and salt in a bowl.
2. Put the butter and confectioners' sugar in a food processor, and process until smooth.
3. Pulse in the egg, vanilla, and lemon zest until combined. Add the flour mixture and process to make a soft buttery dough.
4. Divide dough in half onto 2 (12-inch long) sheets of plastic wrap, using the plastic, shape into rough logs.
5. Refrigerate the dough logs for 30 minutes until just firm enough to shape into uniform logs, 8-inches long by 2-inches in diameter. Refrigerate until firm, at least 2 hours or overnight.
6. Preheat oven to 325 degrees F.
7. Scatter either the sanding sugars or toasted nuts on a work surface and roll the logs until completely coated.
8. Cut into 1/4-inch thick cookies and space about 1 inch apart on parchment-lined baking sheets.
9. Bake until golden around the edges, about 20 to 25 minutes. Cool cookies on the pan on wire racks. Store in an airtight container at room temperature for up to 2 weeks.

Gluten-Free Chocolate Chip Cookies

INGREDIENTS

- ¼ cup vegan margarine
- ½ cup brown sugar
- ½ cup caster sugar
- 1 egg, beaten
- ¾ cup rice flour
- 1 cup soy flour
- 125g dark chocolate, chopped
- 60g additional dark chocolate, melted

DIRECTIONS

1. Beat margarine, sugar and egg in a small bowl with an electric mixer until light and fluffy.
2. Transfer mixture to a large bowl.
3. Stir in sifted flours and chocolate, mix well.
4. Roll tablespoons of mixture into balls.
5. Place 5cm apart onto greased oven trays; flatten slightly.
6. Cook in a moderate oven, for about 20 minutes, or until lightly browned.
7. Stand on tray for 5 minutes; transfer to a wire rack to cool.
8. Decorate cookies by drizzling with extra melted chocolate.

Gluten Free Dutch Sugar Cookies

INGREDIENTS
- 1cup rice flour
- ½cup tapioca flour
- 1cup cornstarch
- 1teaspoon baking powder
- 2 ½teaspoons xanthan gum
- 1teaspoon salt
- 1cup sugar
- 1cup Butter Flavor Crisco
- 1eggs or ¼ cup liquid egg substitute
- 2teaspoons vanilla
- ¼cup potato starch, for kneading

DIRECTIONS
1. Preheat oven to 350 degrees. Have on hand 2 ungreased cookie sheets.
2. In a small bowl, whish together the flour mix, baking powder, xanthan gum, and salt. Set aside.
3. In the bowl of your mixer, cream sugar and crisco. Beat in the egg and vanilla. Add the dry ingredients, mixing enough to combine. The dough will be a soft ball. With your hands, knead in enough of the potato starch to make the dough easy to handle and roll out.
4. Using about half at a time, place a piece of plastic wrap over the ball and roll out to about 1/8 inch thickness.
5. Cut into desired shapes and place on pan.
6. Decorate with coloured sugars before baking or use frosting to decorate after baking.
7. (With this dough, you can use all the scraps.) Just scrape them together and roll out again. They will not get tough.

8. Bake for about 13 minutes. Cool very slightly before removing from the pan.

Flourless Chocolate Snowball Cookies

INGREDIENTS
- ½ cup ground almonds
- ½ cup cocoa powder
- 1 teaspoon baking powder
- ⅛ teaspoon salt
- ¼ cup butter, at room temperature
- ⅔ cup brown sugar
- 1 egg
- ½ teaspoon vanilla
- 4 squares dark chocolate, melted and cooled (112 grams)
- ¼ cup icing sugar

DIRECTIONS
1. Mix first four ingredients in a small bowl.
2. In a separate bowl, cream butter and brown sugar until light and fluffy.
3. Beat in egg and vanilla.
4. Stir in cooled chocolate.
5. Fold in almond mixture until thoroughly combined.
6. Cover and refrigerate until dough is firm; about 10 - 20 minutes.
7. Preheat oven to 350°F Line 2 baking sheets with parchment paper.
8. Place icing sugar in a bowl. Scoop dough with a tablespoon and roll into balls. Coat with icing sugar. Place on baking sheets.
9. Bake 12-14 minutes. Remove sheets from oven and leave for 2 minutes. Cookies will set up a bit firmer as they sit. Remove to a rack to cool completely.

Oatmeal Lace Cookies

INGREDIENTS
- 1 cup sugar
- ½ cup unsalted butter, room temperature
- ¼ cup flour
- 1 tablespoon vanilla extract
- ¼ teaspoon salt
- 1 ½ cups old fashioned oats

DIRECTIONS
1. Preheat oven to 375.
2. Beat sugar and butter until well blended.
3. Beat in flour, vanilla and salt.
4. Stir in oats.
5. Form into a ball. (See photo).
6. Cover and refrigerate cookie dough 1 hour.
7. Line 2 baking sheets with parchment paper.
8. Roll dough by tbsp full between palms into one inch balls. (I cut the dough ball into 24 equal portions, and then roll each portion into a ball.).
9. Place dough balls on baking sheets, spacing 1 1/2 inches apart (cookies will spread during baking).
10. Using bottom of drinking glass as aid, flatten cookies to 1 1/2-inch rounds. (See photo).
11. Bake until cookies are golden brown, about 12 - 13 minutes, turning the cookie sheet once mid-way through baking.
12. Let cookies rest on sheets 1 minute.
13. Using spatula, transfer cookies to a rack and cool completely.

Chocolate Almond Crisps

INGREDIENTS

- 2 cups ground blanched almonds
- 1 $\frac{1}{2}$ cups icing sugar
- 4 tablespoons cocoa powder
- 2 $\frac{1}{2}$ teaspoons ground cinnamon
- $\frac{1}{8}$ teaspoon ground cloves
- 3 ounces unsweetened chocolate
- $\frac{1}{2}$ teaspoon almond extract
- 2 large egg whites

DIRECTIONS

1. Preheat the oven to 325°F.
2. Line a couple of cookie trays with parchment paper.
3. In a food processor, process the almonds with the sugar until finely ground.
4. Add the cocoa, spices and broken up chocolate and process again, until the chocolate is finely ground.
5. Process in the egg whites and the extract until it blends and forms a mass.
6. Remove the dough, let sit for about 5 minutes.
7. Roll out on a board sprinkled with icing sugar.
8. Cut with cookie cutters and place on the trays.
9. Bake in the centre of the oven for 10 to 12 minutes until almost firm and slightly puffed; they should not be browned.
10. Let cool then peel from the paper.

Gingerbread Cookies (Gluten Free)

INGREDIENTS
- 2cups gluten-free flour
- 1teaspoon baking powder
- $\frac{1}{2}$teaspoonbicarbonate of soda
- 1teaspoon cinnamon
- 2teaspoons ground ginger
- 1pinch salt
- 1egg
- 125g butter
- $\frac{1}{4}$cup golden syrup
- $\frac{1}{2}$cup brown sugar

DIRECTIONS
1. In a bowl cream the butter and brown sugar.
2. Add golden syrup and egg and mix till combined.
3. In a seperate bowl sift together all the dry ingredients, then add to the wet ingredients.
4. Mix together and then refrigerate for 1 hour.
5. Remove dough from refrigerator and place onto a floured surface and knead lightly.
6. roll out to 5mm thickness and then cut into shapes using cookie cutters.
7. Bake in 170 degree celsius oven for approx 15 minutes or till well browned.
8. Leave to cool on trays for 5 minutes then transfer to cooking racks.
9. when cool ice with royal icing or any hard setting icing.

www.ingramcontent.com/pod-product-compliance
Lightning Source LLC
Chambersburg PA
CBHW071439070526
44578CB00001B/150